Everyday Life in Victorian America 1865–1900

BY ROBERT H. WALKER

KRIEGER PUBLISHING COMPANY
Malabar, Florida
1994

Original Edition 1967
Reprint Edition 1994 w/ corrections
(Originally entitled Life in the Age of Enterprise)

Printed and Published by
KRIEGER PUBLISHING COMPANY
KRIEGER DRIVE
MALABAR, FLORIDA 32950

Library of Congress Cataloging-In-Publication Data
Walker, Robert Harris, 1924-
    [Everyday life in the age of enterprise, 1865-1900]
    Life in Victorian America, 1865-1900 / by Robert H. Walker.
        p.   cm.
    Previously published: Everyday life in the age of enterprise,
1865-1900.
    Includes index.
    ISBN 0-89464-297-9
    1. United States--Social life and customs--1865-1918--Juvenile
literature. I. Title.
E168.W2   1994
973.8--dc19   88-808
                                                      CIP

10   9   8   7   6   5   4   3   2

Contents

Song covers (above, 1853-1870) reflected topical interest, sentimental attitudes and the associational impulse.

Acknowledgements

My first debt is to the authors of histories, biographies, and special studies from which I borrowed shamelessly and was unable, because of the nature of this work, to credit through the use of footnotes. Three formidable scholars and teachers—Ray A. Billington, Thomas C. Cochran, and Roy F. Nichols—opened many aspects of this era for me as I sat in their lectures. Two graduate assistants, Pastora San Juan and Akiko Murkata, helped me form and illustrate generalizations on several subjects. Miss San Juan searched newspaper files, print collections, and unpublished sources, particularly Elizabeth Steele Wright's manuscript diary in the Library of Congress Manuscript Division. On two difficult subjects, Miss Murakata assembled material from secondary works. Jean Bernard did the Index with her characteristic enthusiasm and alacrity. The George Washington University—Dean Arthur E. Burns and the University Research Committee, and Vice President John Anthony Brown—allowed me time and money for research and writing. The Library of Congress not only furnished the raw materials and a place to belabor them but also offered services that went regularly beyond the essential minimum. I would therefore like especially to thank two chiefs of the Stack and Reader Division, Edward N. MacConomy and Dudley B. Ball, and three members of their staff: Herbert L. Davis, W. D. Boyd, and Larry Shade. Milton Kaplan assisted invaluably in the selection of illustrations, all of which are from the Library of Congress and most of which are from the Division of Prints and Photographs.

Nancy Madden loaned me the engaging manuscript diary (4 vols., 1887–91) of her grandfather, Leon H. Riddle of Marion, Kansas. Philip Emerson let me use his late father's unique scrapbooks of 1890s magazine humor. Ralph H. Gabriel cleared several shelves of his personal library in order to put needed books in my hands. For a couple of long evenings my mother submitted patiently to my cross-questioning on the details of everyday life in the Age of Enterprise as she knew it. Finally, I would like to thank the editor of this series, Louis B. Wright, and Thomas G. MacPherson of Putnam's for their informed guidance.

ROBERT H. WALKER

Everyday Life
in Victorian America
1865–1900

Effects of the scroll saw were in evidence along the roof line of this San Francisco residence built in the 1860s. Other aspects of the "Gingerbread Age" included the stained-glass windowpanes, the carved designs on every visible piece of wood, and the generous cellar door outside the house. (Robert W. Kerrigan photo for Historic American Buildings Survey)

Photograph by H. S. Wyer, 1897.

1 Village Home and Family: 1860s

THE ERA between the close of the Civil War and the
beginning of the twentieth century has attracted a number of unflattering sobriquets. Thinking of the needless errors
of the Reconstruction, one historian called it a "Tragic
Era"; recalling plunder of public treasuries by promoters and
politicians, another named it the "Great Barbecue." Because
of the crudities made manifest by a new technology and a
recently risen industrial middle class, others have written of a
"Chromo Civilization" or a "Gingerbread Age." Optimism
and Victorian reticence were reflected in such phrases as the
"Age of Innocence" and the "Gay Nineties," while the fear
that this had been a time of superficial rather than profound
achievement caused the age to be labled "Gilded" rather
than golden.

Regardless of the interpretive stress placed on this segment
of the American experience, it was impossible to ignore the
degree of change which transformed the nation from its mid-

13

century agricultural isolation with strong regional differences into a more centralized, urban, industrial society with increasing international involvement. The transformation was achieved by an Age of Enterprise which settled the wilderness, founded new towns and mushroomed old ones into cities, constructed a new physical environment from steam, electricity, coal, gas, iron and steel, wrapped the nation in railroad lines and telegraph cables, and produced a way of life that had embarrassingly outgrown its old patterns and institutions. In order to visualize the impact of these changes on the everyday lives of Americans, it will be useful to contrast an urban home and family of the 1890s (Chapter Seven) with their small-town Midwestern counterparts of the late 1860s—a time when three-quarters of the population still lived either on farms or in villages with fewer than 2,500 inhabitants, and when the center of population was somewhere between Chillicothe and Cincinnati.

To approach this village home of the 1860s we would drive a horse and buggy down a dirt-and-gravel street, stop our horse by the cast-iron hitching post, and step onto a conveniently placed stone block whence a wooden sidewalk would lead us through the gate in a cast-iron or wooden-picket fence, past the formal flower bed with its ornamental iron deer, over the roughly mowed lawn, up the wooden steps and onto the front porch. Already we would be in a world much more quiet and restful than it was soon to become. The unpaved streets created dust, but they muffled the passage of hoof and wheel. The house itself was set well back from the street and sheltered by shade trees whose branches needed no trimming to admit a maze of telephone and electric wires. Built possibly of brick or fieldstone, though more likely of wooden shingles or clapboard painted white, the house itself breathed a kind of ungainly contentment.

If this house had been built in 1865, it might differ structurally from its 100-year-older neighbor in only two or three important ways. Lumber mills had proliferated enough by the middle of the century that the newer house would have been constructed of boards and timbers planed and cut at the mill, rather than hand-hewn on the spot. These timbers would be joined by steel-wire nails, instead of wooden pegs, laboriously carpentered joints, or relatively expensive cast-iron nails. Because heating mechanics had improved, and because commercially made glass was becoming cheap and abundant, the newer house would have more and larger windows. Otherwise, this 1865 house could easily have been built decades or even centuries earlier.

Left over from an earlier day would be the cluster of out-buildings we would see if we approached this house from the rear. Among them might easily be a chicken coop and a cowshed, for it was common well into this period for house-wives, even in cities, to depend on the back yard for eggs and milk. Off to one side would be a small barn for the horse and its feed and for the carriage it pulled. At a healthful distance from the back door, at the end of a well-worn path, would be that most easily recognizable of all outbuildings with its half-moon-carved wooden door ajar for purposes of ventilation.

Architecturally distinctive of the houses of this period were the porch and the ornamental woodwork of the scroll saw. The sizes and shapes of porches varied considerably. In the South they tended to adorn both stories and were known as galleries or verandas. In the parts of the Midwest where summers were torid, the porch often extended around three or even four sides of the house, allowing the porch-sitters to chase an elusive breeze to all points of the compass without surrendering shade and protection. The front porch sheltered the main entrance of the house from the elements and provided a place to shed umbrellas and wet clothing. The back porch allowed the women of the house to perform menial chores outdoors in pleasant weather without dressing for the street. In winter the back porch became a refrigerated pantry.

If a porch were added to an older house it was often done

so with the flourish of the newly fashionable scrollwork. Anyone with a taste for elaborately fretted designs of leaves and scrolls, stems and curlicues, could purchase these mass-produced wooden ornaments from his local lumber yard, add them to eaves and cornices, or join them as spandrels to the porch posts and beams. Porch rails and lattices were also susceptible to this kind of design, and the popularity of this ornamental woodwork was sufficient to earn for this era the title of "Gingerbread Age" among the architectural historians. Of course the "gingerbread" often went far beyond a few corners cluttered with scrollwork. The houses which defined the architectural excesses of the era did so by featuring fluted and carved window and door frames and lintels, double-mansarded roofs, corner towers with bowed windows and conical turrets, sculptured chimney pots, and detailed ornamentation in any spot that would bear it. The inspiration for these homes came from no single architectural precedent but borrowed from all in a way that is generally abhorred today under the heading of eclecticism. Most American towns produced a few eye-catching examples of this overelaborate design.

The floor plan of a middle-class home would be predictable. At the bottom level was the cellar, an ill-ventilated hole in the ground with stone walls and an earthen floor. It was barely tall enough to stand in and was used only for storing items unaffected by dampness. It was to the town-dweller what the springhouse was to the farmer, a year-round cold-storage area. As with the springhouse, the outside cellar entrance was protected by a pair of sloping wooden doors, perfect for sliding and reclining, which automatically became the home base for young children's games and idleness.

The first floor had at least four rooms, typically centered around an entrance hall and staircase. Coming in the front door, with eyes still unaccustomed to the interior dimness, a visitor might be startled by the threatening presence of a lurking demon: hydra-headed, cyclops-eyed, and bristling from

This illustration shows the cellar door as a center for semi-supervised recreation. In the right background is another remnant of an earlier day: the back-yard well with levered dipper. (Engraving in *Hearth and Home*, October 25, 1873)

every joint. This demon would in fact be nothing more dangerous than the ornate maple, oak, or cast-iron hatrack. Its many heads would materialize as hats hung from the finial-crowned pegs; its gleaming eye would take the form of a mirror set at a height convenient for a quick check of the departing housewife's bonnet. Umbrellas and canes poked out from racks carved along the bottom, almost hiding the small bench for waiting callers and the marble-topped shelf for receiving calling cards. Opposite the hatrack behind closed doors and drawn shades, lay the showplace of the Victorian house and the room that was least frequently used —the parlor.

To describe the parlor in detail would require the full resources of a decorator's catalog, so overflowing was it with complicated shapes and objects. Festoons of dark, heavy, fringed material swooped langorously from window frames and tumbled over edges of tables and couches. Overhead the

This turn-of-the-century photograph (by George C. Boldt) faithfully depicts the urge to treat interior decoration as a massive attack on all exposed surfaces and to rest only when an ultimate variety of materials and designs had been assembled in the parlor. Except for the method of illumination, this room could have occurred anywhere in the country at any time during the period.

ceiling vibrated with figured paper or floral ornamentation, and from its center hung a chandelier of intricately pressed metal which was to serve first as a true candleholder, next as a gas and finally as an electric fixture. The walls, crowned by carved or fluted molding, hid behind heavy baseboards, door frames, and varnished wooden panels ornamented with either hand-carved or molded leaves and urns. Where the paneling stopped, thick silken wallpaper began, although the profusion of furnishings and hangings sometimes made it difficult to see either. Hangings included tapestries and reproductions of the more sentimental scenes of the masters, but the real favorites of this era were the lushly colored lithographs. The fireplace, the outstanding built-in feature of the parlor, was as pretentious as the family could afford. Faced with marble, it was crowned by a mantel rising two or three tiers in its columned, sculptured magnificence, embracing at eye level an ornate mirror. Underfoot lay a real or imitation oriental rug of profuse color and design.

Victorian furniture shared the characteristics of the gingerbread exteriors: it was mass produced by steam-powered lathes and saws, and it displayed as much complexity of shape and prolixity of ornamentation as could be managed by machine. Sofas and armchairs were thickly upholstered, often tufted and tasseled, and covered with mohair or thick brocaded fabrics. In winter proudly crocheted antimacassars both enhanced their attractiveness to Victorian eyes and protected the original fabric. In summer chintz covers would be fitted on. An ornately carved center table, draped with cloth, would feature the enormous, deeply embossed family Bible, shut with ornamental brass clasps, and used only to record births, marriages, and deaths. Available floor space would be filled with inlaid wooden side chairs, small desks or secretaries, framed paintings displayed on

Scenes like this by John Rogers (1878) not only occupied favored places in Victorian interiors but also showed how leisure was spent in small communities which did not have regular public entertainment. Note the ornately carved table.

easels, or potted greenery set in huge floor vases or hip-level wicker planters. Spool-turned whatnots stood gingerly on the floor, and pierced, lacy étagères hung precariously on the walls. Ranged on their narrow shelves were the family's prized art objects: china and porcelain cups and plates, pewter or silver compotes and urns, glazed ceramic bud vases, and—in the most conspicuous position—a plaster reproduction of one of John Rogers' enduringly popular folksy groups of checkers players, political haranguers, or baby weighers. No wonder the feather duster was perferred to the dustcloth!

Compared with this room, the rest of the house was stark simplicity. Such is the cyclical nature of popular taste that the Victorian family would doubtless have relegated to daily use the less pretentious pieces of Colonial and Federal design which today are valued above the curved and carved monstrosities then so proudly displayed in the parlor. Thus the second parlor, or the sitting room or living room as it came to be called, would have been more congenial to twentieth-century taste. This room might have a plain ceiling with a simple molding, walls either finished in plaster or papered less ornately, and a simpler, cheaper, sturdier carpet. It too might have its potted palms and ferns, its family portraits adorned with the cylindrical pods of cattail reeds, and its colorful lithographs of bucolic scenes and recent disasters. On its larger center table, however, would rest the books, magazines, and newspapers which the family actually read. Around it would be placed father's club chair, mother's rocker, and the slatback chairs the children sat in while studying or playing cards. In its cabinets were stored the games and sewing supplies that came into view each afternoon and evening. The showpiece of this room was the piano, covered with a dark cloth on which the women had hand painted designs in oils. Also in this room was a functioning fireplace or an efficient coal stove, suitably ornate, immaculate in its coat of stove-black, and as popular in the evenings as was the kitchen stove at dawn.

Behind the parlor was the dining room, almost totally filled by the huge oval oak or mahogany table, resting ponderously on a split pedestal or on carved corner legs whose detailed turnings were reflected in the slenderer legs of the chairs surrounding it. For most families this table, with center leaves added, had to seat at least a score of diners on holiday occasions; many a Christmas dinner had to be served in shifts. Space also was needed for the buffets, breakfronts, and cabinets which stored flatware, linen, and china, and which held the serving dishes during those generous meals. A Victorian table, set for festive eating, was something to behold. The best linen napery glistened like dry snow; the heavy glass or crystal tumblers mirrored the painstakingly polished heavy-handled silverplated place settings; platters with scalloped edges revealed floral designs or historic scenes; serving dishes combined the details of classic and roccoco design in handles and lids. Vases of artificial flowers and dishes of wax fruit added still more color but could

Advertisements of the period illustrated the advanced state of the lithographer's art (this one was by O. Poleni, 1874) and the penchant for comic "before and after" appeals to the buyer. Taste for the ornate can be seen in the crosshatchings, the half-relief figures, and the urn at the top.

Although this kitchen was modernized to the extent of hot running water, the bucket and coal scuttle show that fetching and carrying were still an intimate part of household routines. (Lithograph by L. Prang, 1874)

hardly compete with the inimitable tan of a baked fowl or the rich dark brown of a well-turned roast.

Behind the sitting room was the kitchen, which also adjoined the dining room, sometimes via a serving pantry which stored both food and utensils. The kitchen also gave onto a back porch; a large window commanded the backyard and admitted plenty of daylight. The remaining wall space was monopolized by an enormous wood or coal stove, often set into an interior brick wall which served both to insulate it from the wooden studs and to enclose the flue. To the stove was often attached a water tank with coils placed near the fire box, and pipes leading to faucets over an adjacent sink. In this form hot running water first entered many American homes. Usually, however, the kitchen sink was simply a zinc trough resting in a low cabinet that had to be filled from a kettle and emptied by being lifted out of its frame and dumped off the back porch.

Kettles stood ever ready on the stove, pans hung from hooks on the walls, a small table for the family's informal meals might be more or less permanently set. Pails stood by the door for fetching coal and water. The housewife rolled her dough for pastries on a marble- or metal-topped table, whitened by its constant contact with flour; for chopping and butchering she had another table finished in wood thick and hard enough to withstand the cleaver and the blade. Among her prized gadgets she numbered an apple corer, invaluable at harvest time; some new pressed-metal utensils for grating, shredding, and peeling; and one of the many varieties of patented ice boxes always newly on the market. The air of the kitchen, tinged with the pungency of woodsmoke or the acrid hint of burning coal, made fragrant with the aroma of baking bread, carried the warm associations of family life, the intimate routines of chores and morning meals. This room was, however, the unchallenged domain of the house-

These children were too dressed up for most small town schools but they were anticipating one of the universal childhood pleasures of these decades. (Photo by Frances B. Johnston, 189?)

wife and her girl; and they looked with proud satisfaction from the pan bottoms gleaming on the wall to the unfinished wooden floor, bleached by the scrubbrush and indented into the familiar paths of use.

These four rooms completed the desired minimum for the first floor. If there were more space, it was likely to become a library or a study where the head of the house installed a rolltop desk at which he posted the family books, and a leather chair where he smoked his pipes and dozed peacefully on Sunday afternoons. A nearby table held tobacco cannister, pipe rack, and a few issues of sporting magazines placed tactfully over the latest *Police Gazette*. Bookshelves housed the matched sets of Dickens, Scott, and Bulwer-Lytton; Parson Weems' *The Life of George Washington;* and almanacs for several years back.

Dominating the second floor was the master bedroom containing whatever showpieces the family possessed in the way of dressers, wardrobes, and bureaus. On the washstand stood a porcelain pitcher and bowl, ornamented with a floral design or pastel pastoral scene; on the dressing table stood rows of cosmetic jars in embroidered covers, lint brushes, and a silver comb, brush, and mirror set. In those days of long-haired fashions, the housewife would pass many hours seated at this table, applying the standard 100 brush strokes to her waist-long locks. The furniture itself, like that in the parlor, would have been factory-made of carved dark woods or veneers. Only the bed frame might be of cast iron, since, of the many varieties of metal furniture sold in midcentury America, garden furniture and bed frames remained popular. If there was a fireplace in use on the second floor, it would surely be the one in the master bedroom, a room that sometimes doubled as sitting room for the old folks on evenings when the young folks had taken over the first floor. If the house was heated with stoves, it was usual to pass the flue from the sitting-room stove through the master bedroom, thereby making use of the escaping heat.

The other bedrooms, usually two or three, were smaller, colder, and less pretentious versions of the master bedroom. Their decor, of course, depended on whether they housed male or female children, or some older relative. The second-best bedroom was frequently kept as a guest room during an age when protracted visits were common. Its bed undoubtedly displayed the housewife's finest crocheted or quilted bedspread and a knitted afghan folded at the foot. On the floor rested a prized hooked rug. When guests were not in residence this became a sewing room and, as central heating made the upstairs habitable even in winter, the sewing machine was moved here permanently from the sitting room.

Victorian bedroom furniture differed from today's in only three important ways. The washstand, or commode, an essential item in the days before indoor plumbing, lingered throughout the century as a showpiece if not a necessity. With the turn of the century came a tendency to build closets into the bedrooms; as this happened the mammoth mirror-fronted wardrobe disappeared into the attic. Finally, the bed itself underwent an evolution. When ceilings were high and floors were cold, there was every reason to have a sleeping surface three or four feet off the floor and ornamented headboards and posts ascending toward the ceiling. Since then the head- and footboards have simplified, shrunk, and all but disappeared, the bed has gotten lower and lower, and modern coil springs and mattresses support the body's weight a great deal more evenly than did the hammock-like mesh springs and stuffed mattresses of that day.

Above the bedroom level was a half-finished half story called the attic. It was reached by a plain narrow staircase and served as an important seasonal storage area where trunks in summer were packed with mothballs and winter woolens. A storehouse of discarded and not-quite-useless items, the attic became a children's museum filled with the charm of the unfamiliar. Sometimes a population explosion, or the need for servant quarters, would force a family to convert the attic to additional sleeping quarters; but without modern insulation, electric fans, or central heat, the attic climate was far from ideal in either summer or winter.

Having inspected the setting we can imagine a cast of characters. According to census figures, the average size of a household in the 1860s and '70s was slightly more than five persons. In rural areas families were larger; in the cities, smaller. In a town family, then, we could expect two or three children who had survived infancy. In those days of the extended family, furthermore, it would not be at all unlikely to find a grandparent whose spouse had died and who had then moved in with one of the children; even aunts and uncles found homes with nieces and nephews if there were no closer relative who could support them. If the family had even a moderate middle-class income, it would also be logical to expect to find a hired girl who lived in the home throughout most of the year. This girl might be the daughter of relatives or friends who were not so well off. She might be part of a large farm family who could spare a daughter in the hope that she would get the advantages of town life and a refined home. She might be the child of immigrant parents who used servitude as a means of instilling a good command of English. Depending on her relationship to her employers, she would be more or less a part of the family and treated as a servant only in some respects. She would have little in common with a city maid who appeared for work each morning, returned to her own home at night, and remained outside the social life of the family she served.

Day began for this family with the hired girl tumbling out of bed in the early light, already clad in long underwear if the season were cold, slipping quickly into a flannel robe, and racing to the kitchen to kindle the stove fire. Once there she would complete her dressing while the kettles heated the cooking and washing water, check the breakfast table she had set the night before, and begin her cooking. Soon the early riser would be joined in the kitchen by the rest of the family. In mild weather, each would wash from the pitcher and bowl in his bedroom, dress, turn down the bedclothes and open the windows wide before coming down to breakfast. In winter, however, the water in the pitcher would be skimmed with ice and the room itself far too chilly for unclad comfort. Hence it was common to leave clothes in the kitchen the night before, so that on rising one could descend to the warmth of the kitchen stove, dress as near to it as possible, and wash in stove-warmed water. If father was a man who shaved himself, he would of course get first claim to the hot water and to a position near the stove where he could brush up his lather, strop his straight razor, and apply it smartly to his cheeks and chin. Happily for the mistress of the kitchen, she need not surrender shaving space every day. Many men grew mustaches, sideburns or beards. Others preferred the sociability of the barber shop and the luxury of a ten-cent shave to the early-morning confusion of the kitchen; and, in the days before some blade manufacturer made men fear the "five o'clock shadow," a "cleanshaven man" was one who shaved twice a week.

To the accompaniment of dressing and ablution, the girl would prepare a breakfast of smoked pork or beef, potatoes, toast and coffee. Children, accompanied by the inevitable reminders and reprimands, would soon be off on foot toward school. Father, his departure delayed the length of an after-breakfast cigar, would then begin his walk to work, leaving the house to the women. They would have a busy morning in store. The girl's first job was to visit each bedroom, empty and rinse the chamber pots, and refill the pitchers. After the early-morning airing, the windows must be closed, beds made, and clothes put away. Then there were the breakfast dishes and the preparation for the principal meal of the day. Daily chores included dusting and sweeping, and washing the delicate chimneys of the kerosene lamps. If it was Monday, laundry would be done with the aid of a scrubboard or a hand-cranked ancestor of the electric washer and wringer.

Village and rural schools like this one often mixed students aged 7 to 17 in a single room. See page 115. (Photo by Strohmeyer & Wyman, 1899)

Tuesday and Wednesday meant ironing with flatirons heated on the stove but made more easily managed through the development of handles which could be detached from the iron and therefore would not become too hot to touch while the iron itself was heating. Thursday, the traditional girl's day off, had no inevitable chore; but Friday meant special attention to housecleaning, and Saturday brought the extra chore of baking for two days.

While the girl was bearing the principal burden of these chores, the housewife would have donned her hat and cape, looped a wicker basket over her arm, and walked to market for her daily shopping. This stroll to market was to the housewife what the time in the barber chair was to her husband. It was then that she met friends and neighbors, exchanged what passed for news, and contributed her share to the common pool of personal history that men scoffingly called gossip. With no pink giant of a refrigerator-freezer to preserve quantities of food at home, however, her need to market daily was quite legitimate; and, with basket heavy, she hurried back to assist the girl in preparing the freshly bought food for dinner.

This heavy noonday meal was served in the dining room on a white linen tablecloth with napkins preserved in individualized napkin rings to avoid the need for washing them daily. Soup, meat, potatoes, rolls, and pie were the unchanging features of this meal; other dishes varied with the season. Fruits and vegetables, some from the back-yard garden, were enjoyed abundantly while in season but were otherwise scarce. Apples, individually wrapped, could be savored fresh through the long winter as they emerged from the basement barrel. Other fruits and some vegetables were regularly preserved in their own juices, pickled and served as relishes, made into jellies and jams, or dried like raisins and prunes. An 1865 dinner would have seemed starchy to modern tastes; and, although the table would have been laden with a surprising number of dishes, the menu for a week or a month offered little variety. The atmosphere at the dinner table tended to be rather formal. Children spoke when spoken to and recited rather than conversed as their parents queried them. It was here that decorum was learned, table etiquette instilled, and family policy set forth.

Refreshed by a short stretch on the sofa, the father walked back to work and the boys to school. Girls often attended morning sessions only, remaining home in the afternoons. Unless there were some special ritual in progress—spring housecleaning, fall canning—the women were very likely to spend their afternoons with needle and thread. The sewing group included daughters home from school, the hired girl as soon as she had finished the dinner dishes and cleaned the kitchen, any female relatives living with the family, the mother, who had changed into a more formal dress, and frequently a housewife or two from the neighborhood. Home weaving had become rare by this period, but needlework still meant a great deal more than darning socks and sewing on buttons. For, although the fabrics were purchased rather than homemade, they were still typically sewn into garments in the home. In a good-sized town, a housewife might rely on a tailor or dressmaker to supply the pattern and cut the cloth for a suit before she herself did the sewing. Shirts, blouses, undergarments, summer dresses, and children's clothes were often made completely in the home from magazine and mail-order patterns, or else by the time-honored method of measure, fit, and try again.

The next predictable event was "tea," a substantial meal of meat, vegetables, and fruits, served some time between 5:30 and 7:00 P.M. As diet consciousness grew, this meal became lighter. In summer it might consist entirely of cold dishes: potato salad, cold cuts and sausages, and fresh fruit for dessert. In most parts of the country—and to less pretentious people everywhere—this meal soon became known as supper. Most nights of the year the whole family assembled after supper in the living room around the large table which held the household's most efficient lamp (the fanciest would be in the parlor). Here the children did their lessons, father read the paper, and mother went on with her sewing. At some point, father might put down his paper, and pick up the family Bible for the reading of a daily verse. If there were both a daughter and a piano, and very likely there were, the stillness would be broken by scales and arpeggios, followed —after lessons—by group singing of hymns or an occasional "Tenting Tonight," "Oh! Susanna," and other Civil War and minstrel favorites. If there were a guest in the house, the daughter would be proudly summoned to perform a Brahms minuet, a Mozart étude, or some other carefully rehearsed "piece." American families went in heavily for music. Many a home boasted its own string quartet; church choirs and glee clubs claimed hours of assiduous practice from their willing members.

There were other forms of indoor recreation, many of them—card games, backgammon, dominoes, chess, checkers —still popular today. Especially associated with this era was a family of gadgets made to illuminate views and illustrations, and known loosely as "magic lanterns." If they pro-

duced a three-dimensional effect they were called stereo-
scoptions, or stereopticons. These machines were used
mainly to bring into the living room the beauties of man-
made art or of remote nature and, like much recreation enjoyed during the late nineteenth century, they were deliberately instructive as well as entertaining. The stereopticon
offered not only a short course in art history, or a world
travelog, but also a view of the South's progress under Reconstruction. Many of the profitable paperbound books of
this era had to do with self-improvement of one kind or another. Maps came bound with panoramic views giving dimensions to geography as well as history. Correspondence
courses flourished. Even card games reflected this trend.
Some homes today still boast a packet of "author cards" with
which can be played a game based on the knowledge of
which authors wrote what works; but most of our card games
today depend only on skill and chance within an internalized
set of rules. In a Gilded Age home, however, it would have
been far from surprising if a guest were invited to sit down
for a friendly game of Artists, Musical Composers, or Shakespeare—all of which demanded external knowledge. Other
card games imparted incidental lore about ornithology,
mythology and general history.

The long days of summer brought the family out of doors
in the evenings and removed them from the pressures of self-
improvement. From the barn loft came a set of wicker furniture—including a two-passenger swing—for the wide front
porch, and a few cast-iron pieces for the lawn. The iron
furniture took the form of intricately designed, uncomfort-
ably low-backed settees, sometimes fashioned in a circular
mold so as to fit around the trunk of a tree. Between conveniently placed trees a hammock might be strung. After
supper would be heard the syncopated clink of horseshoe
against horseshoe, and occasionally against the peg, as the
men and boys tested their pitching prowess. As the light
faded a mandolin or banjo might appear along with a pitcher

of cold lemonade; complaints would be heard against the heat, the drought, and the mosquitoes; the porch swing would begin to creak an accompaniment to the subdued remarks of a daughter and her caller, who happily made the best of the chaperoned intimacy of the family.

What marked a back-yard scene as distinctively post-Civil War was the presence of wickets and pegs, gaily striped mallets and round wooden balls. The intensity of the croquet craze was comparable only to the invasion of the bicycle, which was soon to follow. Sets were installed with candles set atop the wickets so that play could go on into the night. Lawnless families traveled miles to play on a neighbor's court; towns organized teams and played matches. But croquet was more than just another fad; it was the first popular outdoor game designed for equal participation by both sexes. No great size or strength was required to wield the slender mallets; in fact the manuals of the game advised women how to assume graceful and pleasing attitudes while stroking the ball. Women's fashions soon took note of the opportunity for exposing a well-shod ankle while the young lady placed her foot on her own ball and "sent" her opponent's ball behind the peach tree. Titillated by the possible romantic consequences of this recreational mingling of the sexes, Victorian Americans saw croquet as an avenue to the heart. A popular song of the late 1860s told of a maid and youth seated side by side as the "mallets and balls unheeded lay . . . and I thought to myself, is that Croquet?"

Weekend routines differed from weekdays in some notable respects. Saturday was likely to be the busiest day for everyone in the family. The breadwinner in a small town probably earned his bread by serving the farm community in some respect: selling feed and supplies, buying produce, arranging for shipment or credit. Since Saturday was the traditional farmer's day in town, the father doubtless went to work earlier and stayed later than usual, caught in Saturday's bustle. The housewife and the girl, assisted by the children, did a thorough job of housecleaning and a double load of cooking in preparation for the Sabbath. Boys, freed from school, were saddled with wood-chopping, cleaning the ashes from stoves and hearths, polishing boots, carrying water, raking leaves, cleaning yards and outbuildings. Still, with luck, they would manage a half day of hiking, sledding or swimming in season. There were plenty of vacant lots for pick-up versions of the newly popular game of baseball, and nature—in the form of fish and game—was a lot more accessible then than now.

Saturday night might well have meant an evening at the theater or in the home of friends, but Sunday was a day for family, church, and tranquillity. The whole family, dressed its best, went forth to a rather long morning church service. Dinner, served from foods prepared on Saturday, was followed by a nap; the exchange of visits with other branches of the family; reading, letter writing, or other quiet and inconspicuous diversions. While the younger children stayed at home, the older ones and their parents attended an evening church service, after which courting couples would break the day's strict family solidarity by walking home together.

There were several reasons for the preservation of this old-fashioned pattern of weekend life. In the first place, most American families were habitually and sentimentally bound to the tradition of the religious Sabbath, a Lord's Day that was meant to resemble the rest of the week as little as possible. In the second place, this refreshing break from the routines of weekdays was a matter of considerable convenience. With the hired girl spending the day with her own family, the housewife was interested in minimizing cooking and housework; and a hot Sunday could be made a lot more bearable indoors if the stove need not be lit. Also, in this day of strong family feelings, a day was needed for the exchange of news, for distributing congratulations, and for arranging help for those who needed it.

Into this weekly pattern intruded a number of major interruptions: some seasonal, some predictable, and some casual. Of these the most terrifying was an annual rite so formidable that its very mention unnerved men generations removed from its heyday. Its name was spring cleaning, and its annual occurrence was something clever men avoided by a well-timed fishing, hunting or even business trip. For those who did not escape, it proved a ruthless event. It began with the moving of every fixture or piece of furniture in the house, either outdoors or out of the way. With the floors cleared, the carpet tacks were pulled and the rug hung on a back-yard line where it was mercilessly beaten with a wooden-handled wire loop designed for that express torture to dusty-eyed man and tormented fabric. The straw that had formed the pad under the rug was burned, the floor scrubbed and needlessly polished, fresh straw laid, and the beaten rug tacked down again. Upholstered furniture was aired and beaten, wood surfaces were dusted and oiled, fireplaces and stoves were flushed out, stairs and bannisters were waxed, cabinets, shelves, and closets emptied and cleaned. The house, in short, was almost literally turned upside down, spanked and burnished, and put back into something like its original order. The ritual was timed to coincide with the moment when winter heat could be dispensed with and the house relieved of its seasonal grime. It was also taken as an opportunity for collecting, cleaning and repairing the family's winter wardrobe, and storing it in the attic ready for instant use next fall.

The ritual of canning foods was not quite so uncompromising, but it was another time when men and boys conspired to be elsewhere if they could. Canning had to be closely timed with the height of a season, when the food was cheap, abundant and fully ripe. Preparing and cleaning the food itself was often a major part of the labor—shelling peas, husking corn—while simultaneously scores of jars and their lids were poked about in boiling water. The food was then cooked in huge vats, strained and drained. With spices and preservatives added, it was placed in the gleaming jars, and sealed over with molten paraffin—another messy job— before the jars were lidded. However much the men of the house might dread those days when the kitchen became a cannery, when pots steamed day and night, and when the usual services of the house were dismissed with a wave, they nonetheless valued highly the end products which adorned their tables throughout the year and which provided the only relief from meat, potatoes, and bread when fresh produce was not locally in season.

Of the many holidays which broke normal routines throughout the year, three were centered in church and home: Easter, Thanksgiving, and Christmas. They all involved appropriate church decorations and services of prayer and praise. What happened in the home on these holidays would be largely familiar to a visitor from the 1960s. During Easter week, eggs were boiled and colored and candy gifts were given. On Thanksgiving, the harvest was celebrated

The enormously popular, sentimental Currier & Ives lithographs symbolized the nostalgic, family-centered meaning of occasions like Thanksgiving. (1867)

HOME TO THANKSGIVING.

with gifts to the poor and turkey and trimmings for the family. Christmas was not so commercial or so prolonged as it has since become. Gifts were simple, utilitarian, and often homemade. They included clothing and small manufactured objects—a jackknife, a doll—and stressed foods such as oranges and coconut which today would be considered too commonplace for gifts. But many other things would have been familiar. Since Thomas Nast's cartoons during the Civil War, the plump jolly figure of St. Nicholas had come to symbolize the generosity of the season. The Northern European custom of cutting an evergreen and bringing it indoors was spreading even to the western part of the country where Spanish customs had originally been more prevalent. The tree was trimmed with candles and strings of beads, berries, and popped corn. Locked behind parlor doors, it was surreptitiously underlaid with gifts which, the children concluded, could only have been placed there by a chimney-shooting saint. As with Easter and Thanksgiving, a family feast was part of the day, featuring special treats like citrons, raisins, nuts, homemade candy and preserves. Housewives would decorate their homes with lilies, cornstalks and pumpkins, or holly and mistletoe. From a modern point of view, these holidays seem altogether less public, communal, and commercial than they have become. The home provided their central focus, and they existed principally as occasions for the members of the family to give pleasure and reassurance to one another.

Not only were holidays more home-centered then than now, but so were the activities surrounding the essential life processes: courtship and marriage, birth, education, sickness and death. Of course young people want and need to get off by themselves, and they have always found ways to do so. But in the small town of the 1860s there were very few public places to which a young man could escort a young lady. The result was that, especially in unpleasant weather, the suitor spent a great deal of time in his young lady's home.

The winter equivalent of the porch swing was the parlor sofa to which the daughter and her caller might adjourn, albeit well within sight and sound of the family. Often the caller would join in family activities in the living room: the singing, card games, or magic-lantern diversions. If the interest grew at all serious, the young lady might soon be appearing as a regular guest at Sunday dinners or suppers in the young man's home. As the courtship neared a climax the young man really would beard the girl's father in his den on a Sunday afternoon, announce the seriousness of his intentions, and surprise no one by requesting his daughter's hand. On some occasions the father would refuse, and would have a much better chance of making his disapproval stick than he would today.

If the answers came out yes all around, the two families and their close friends would hear the news at a small party in the home that was about to lose a daughter, and preparations for the wedding would begin. For the most part, these preparations meant accelerated needlework for the female relatives of the bride, since it was their obligation to provide a trousseau. Dressing the lady and equipping her home were projects limited only by family resources. Not only the bridal gown itself, but quantities of dresses and underclothing for daily and special wear were also accumulated: embroidered slips, elegant nightcaps, plain and fancy stockings, bonnets for all occasions, and even feathers and mantillas. A portion of the family's good European lace would go with the bride as would a share of the jewelry, although it was generally considered the groom's prerogative to present the bride with jewels. If he could not afford anything glittering, he could offer his intended an ivory fan, a dainty watch, or some finely wrought object for her toilet table.

Early-morning wedding ceremonies were quite common, but the early hour was no deterrent to whatever elegance the families could afford. A modest affair might find the bride in colored silk and the groom in a business suit; but the bride with means preferred a lace-covered white gown of satin or rich moire and a bevy of bridesmaids attired nearly as impressively. A carriage would bring the bride and her maids to the church; the groom and his party, in striped trousers and morning coats, waited at the door. After the familiar service the guests would assemble for the wedding breakfast at the bride's home where turkey, ham, tongue and possibly wine or cider would be served. In the center of the breakfast table stood a magnificent cake surrounded by orange blossoms. As the cake was cut, the family's honored friend proposed the bride's health; the father of the bride toasted the groom, who returned in kind, and the party was under way.

Sometime during the confusion the bride would change to street clothes and prepare to leave on the wedding trip if she were lucky enough to have one. Honeymoons were considered more of a luxury than a routine; they tended to be short and arranged so as not to interfere with the bridegroom's work. Either on their wedding night or on their return from the honeymoon, the newlyweds would be honored with a ritual that has survived only in the form of a few tin cans tied to an automobile bumper. The young men who knew the couple would assemble an arsenal of pots, pans, gravel, spoiled produce, and proceed to manufacture a night of noise and nuisance. Following the couple to their new home as raucously as possible, and fortified by portable refreshment, they would keep up a stream of loud songs, hurtling fruit and stones, and general mischief far into the night. They called this the charivari. After the exuberance surrounding the wedding, the couple would be paid a series of polite calls. During their first year as man and wife, they would be the guests of honor at dinner parties, perhaps conceived in order to minimize the strain on the bride's kitchen skills.

In an era when doctors, trained nurses, and well-equipped hospitals were still relatively scarce, childbearing and the treatment of sickness typically took place in the home. An ailing member of the family was bundled up in bed in the guest room or in winter on a daybed in the living room, and home remedies were applied: hot and cold compresses, immersion of the feet in hot water, drinking of special teas and herb brews—remedies that had not changed much for centuries. This was indeed the age of Louis Pasteur, Robert Koch, G. T. A. Gaffky, Friedrich Löffler and other men of medical science who were making remarkable advances in germ and microbe theory, in isolating causes and in developing the scientific treatment of disease. But it was still an age when the editor of a leading woman's magazine could claim that dizziness, unsettled nerves, and female disorders could be cured by sleeping with the head of the bed northward. It was possible to pick up a single issue of *Frank Leslie's Illustrated Newspaper,* one of the large-circulation national weeklies, and find advertisements for Hostetter's Celebrated Stomach Bitters, made of "pure Essence of Rye," which could cure "Dyspepsia and all its kindred complaints"; for Reddings' Russia Salve, which cured "all kinds of Sores, Cuts, Scalds, Burns, Boils, Ulcers, Salt Rheum, Erysipelas, Sties, Piles, Corns, Sore Lips, Sore Eyes, etc., etc. . . . as if by Magic"; for the Peruvian Syrup by which "Thousands have been changed . . . from Weak, Sickly, Suffering Creatures, to Strong, Healthy, and Happy Men and Women (the proof of which will be sent free by mail), and Invalids cannot reasonably hesitate to try it"; for a ten-cent booklet listing specific remedies for all imaginable ailments; or, best of all, for Dr. Talbot's Concentrate Medical Pineapple Cider, which, for three dollars a year, could keep its imbibers from ever having any of the diseases for which Hostetter, Redding, and the others promised cures.

Only when home and patent remedies had failed was the doctor summoned, and his arrival was a signal for concern. Neighbors responded with prepared foods, with offers to attend the ailing one, and with the inevitable morsels of advice and recountings of personal experience. If the "ailment" were pregnancy, the routine did not differ much. Lying in, both before and after delivery, was done at home with neighbors taking up the confined mother's chores. A doctor would assist at the delivery, although in some isolated communities this function was still performed by a midwife. The arrival of an infant—especially the couple's first—was the occasion for lavish gifts: hand-sewn and knitted booties, blankets, bonnets and wrappers.

Ever hypochondriacal, Americans in this era had their unique collection of fads and fetishes that supposedly promoted health and vigor. Their most notable penchant was for ventilation, a rather strange fad in the homes where great streams of inside air were constantly being expelled through chimneys and replaced by the air drawn in around door and window frames. Yet homebuilders were encouraged to include skylights to be left constantly open as an exhaust for "used" air. The last to bed was to air the living room before retiring, and daily household routines placed ventilation above all else. It was also an era impressed with the salubrious effects of minerals. Patent medicines and spring tonics promised to restore iron to the blood, and many of the fashionable water-

Scenes such as this were a lot more common than in the twentieth-century America of hospitals and nursing homes. Also exemplified in this scene was the concern of lodge members for their brethren (note the Odd Fellows plaques on the wall). See page 141. (Lithograph by American Oleo Co., 1877)

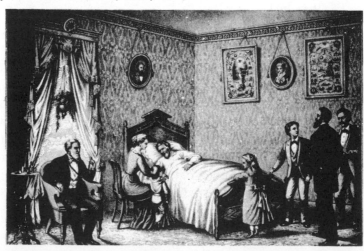

ing places of the day owed their popularity to the medicinal reputation of their mineral springs. Although bloodletting had lost its popularity, the purge was still considered a sovereign remedy, and such natural laxatives as bran, prunes, and sauerkraut were served with, and for, regularity.

When medicines and fresh air failed, death came in the home. The absence of funeral parlors in many communities meant that the family and the neighbors shared the duties of washing the body and preparing it for burial. A mild kind of wake consisted of sitting up with the body during the first nights after death; callers were received and served food prepared by neighbors. A casket was ordered, either from the furniture store or the cabinetmaker; the deceased was laid out in the parlor in a best suit or dress; flowers from friends and neighbors were augmented by a five-dollar wreath from father's lodge. Black-edged cards in shop windows announced the place and time of the funeral. White-gloved pallbearers, followed by black-clad ladies, carried the casket to the church where a lengthy eulogy and lugubrious hymns preceded the procession to the graveside where another attenuated ceremony took place. Returning home, the bereaved family found their house had been cleaned and supplied with food for the next few days.

A center of activity from birth through death, the home inevitably served as schoolhouse to an extent that has not carried over into modern life. Things that were considered vital for girls to learn were almost completely entrusted to their mothers or to the other women in the home. It was here that they learned the arts and sciences of home management, from cooking and sewing to buying and decorating. How to dress, how to behave toward the opposite sex, and how to raise a family were all taught in the home by example and by lecture. For young men the case was not quite the same, especially in an era when modes of earning a living were changing rapidly and when geographical and economic frontiers stimulated mobility. The apprentice system of teaching a boy a trade was more common on the farm than in the towns; still many young Americans acquired the training that was to bring them life-long income by tending their father's store, accompanying him on his selling or buying trips to surrounding farms, distributing type in his printing shop, tending the machines at his factory, or even reading in his law office.

What both sexes invariably acquired at home was moral and social training: ethics and etiquette. The standards and behavior dispensed in the Victorian home were, by modern standards, spectacularly rigid. Right and wrong were clearly divided by heavy lines of Bible-based custom. Punishment for childish misdemeanors—a petty theft, a rowdy evening— seems to have been as severe as in Puritan homes 200 years earlier. Not only was a fundamental Christian morality applied, but it was reinforced by a strain of prudery distinctive enough to have earned the title "Victorianism." Clothing covered all, disguised much, and left little room for freedom of movement. Vocabulary was stilted to avoid the realities, sometimes beyond belief. There was the story of a finishing school which cautioned its young ladies to refer to piano "limbs," rather than legs, and where these very pieces of hardwood were covered with dainty draperies to shield them from view. Delicacy and restraint were the watchwords. If a young lady were complimented on her gown, it might easily mean that she had overdressed and thereby called undue attention to herself. For a man, a modest intaglio ring was recommended above precious stones.

The etiquette of the period was unrelenting. Although many of its absurdities never really penetrated small-town America, it was still expected that young people would "sir" their elders, that men would greet ladies with a full doff instead of a mere tip of the hat, and that a man who was gauche enough to smoke a cigar in public would toss it promptly to the ground upon entering into conversation with a lady. To a proper Victorian such observances constituted

not merely polite behavior but right behavior, as these words
from an etiquette book of the period made clear:

> To a certain extent the observance of the laws of eti-
> quette *is* a matter of morals. They are really the outgrowth
> of kindness, of the feeling of the majority of the refined
> and cultivated people of all nations that whatever tends
> to produce the least friction in social intercourses brings
> the greatest amount of happiness, and, therefore, higher
> morality.

A product of this representative home and family might
seem rigidly predictable today. Dressed rather thoroughly
from the tip of his toe to his Adam's apple, hidden behind a
hedge of whiskers, he might bore us with the merits of his five-
dollar watch tucked firmly in his waistcoat or his celebration
of either the "last cause" of Southern nationalism or the virtues of the party that had saved the Union and freed the
slaves. Constrained by both Puritan morals and Victorian
manners, he might appear orotund, inhibited, and overly
genteel. His stability came from his reliance on church,
home, and family; he was proud of his home town and of his
national past. Yet he trusted firmly his individual conscience
even when it led him away from his neighbors; he saw an
even better town over the horizon; and he believed more in
an America of the future than in an America of the past. It
was lucky he did; for in 1870 he beheld before him a generation of change more radical than he could have imagined.

Engraving after photograph at the Centennial in *Harper's Weekly,*
December 9, 1876.

2 The Impact of Technology

THE MOST evident changes in American life could be
attributed to a group of men loosely called scientists, who
were really more tinkerers than thinkers. Compared with
their European contemporaries they did not contribute
impressively to the accumulation of theoretical explana-
tions of nature's laws; they did excel at applying scientific principles to particular problems: stopping a train,
lighting the darkness, reproducing the human voice at a distance. These inventors, abetted by engineers and industrial
entrepreneurs, drastically altered the human environment
and created a whole new set of possibilities and problems.

The most basic thing they achieved was making man more
powerful. At midcentury man was master of the wind and
the horse that turned his mill and pulled his plow. Water
power he had harnessed in some factories and mills; but
except for a modest fleet of steamships and a large army of
wood-burning locomotives, he had not advanced far beyond

his earliest efforts at controlling the power inherent in nature. By 1900, however, he had mastered the mechanical equivalent of 65,000,000 horses. Four million units of this new power eased the farmers' burdens. Railroads accounted for 24,000,000 horsepower as contrasted with less than 2,000,000 in 1860, and the stage had been set for automotive power to become the dominant prime mover by 1910.

Yet the greatest change in the creation of energy came not from the direct use of steam or internal-combustion engines, but rather as the fulfillment of the prophecy contained in Thomas Eubank's 1849 patent-office report. He wrote of a new force that was "ordained to effect the mightiest revolution in human affairs," a force that could be "drawn rapidly from its hiding place, and made to propel land and water chariots, animate manufacturing mechanisms, become an agricultural laborer, and a household drudge of all our work." The subject of this quaintly worded vision was electricity; its revolutionary character lay in its portability. No longer must a factory be at the waterfall's edge in order to use its energy; no longer must a vehicle carry a weighty supply of fuel and water to be converted into steam; no longer must artificial light be drawn only from immediately adjacent reservoirs of liquids or gases. Carrying current generated miles away, electrical wires and storage batteries brought power conveniently to the job at hand.

The first widespread application of electrical power was to the creation of light. In 1877 the Nicholas Longworths of Cincinnati were hailed as the first family to light their home with electrical arc lights; the next year John Wanamaker's Philadelphia department store used arc lights to make night shopping a new vogue, and by 1880 cities were arc-lighting their busier streets. In spite of the wiring innovations of Charles F. Brush, the creation of light by jumping an electric arc between two sticks of carbon was a noisy and erratic means of illumination. The current sizzled and crackled; the carbon gap required constant adjustment; and the light was too intense for many domestic uses. In answer to these problems Thomas Edison, after years of searching for a suitable filament, patented an incandescent vacuum bulb in 1880. Discovering also how to turn off a single light without affecting an entire system, he provided the necessary basis for a fast-spreading technological revolution which turned on 25,-000,000 lights in the America of 1900.

On the heels of electric light came electrically powered transportation. Richmond, Virginia, claimed the first extensive trolley system (1888), and many communities followed in quick pursuit. The city of Washington carried visitors from train station to hotel in "electric horses"; St. Paul used an electric snowplow in 1891; St. Louis in 1892 installed electric mail cars; New York City boasted 300 electric taxis; and by 1900 the United States had fifteen times as many miles of electrified railways as Canada, England, France, and Russia combined.

The fundamental importance of the electrical revolution, however, was in its application to industrial use. For this potential to be realized a good many innovations were needed: better techniques in the construction of power lines and cables; the introduction of alternating current to succeed direct current as a superior form in which to transport electric power; the perfection of such essential devices as transformers, generators, dynamos, and motors. Most of these innovations were achieved in the 1880s and '90s; although, as recent power failures have reminded us, the electrical art is still far from an exact science. Alternating current won its battle over direct current in the early '90s; during these same years electric motors were developed sufficiently for many industrial uses; Niagara Falls was converted into a source of electric power in 1895. With electrical engineering schools sprouting faster than telegraph poles, the electrical age was well under way by the end of the century. Whereas the census of 1880 had listed no electrical energy as a power source for prime movers, in 1900 it counted 2,500,000 horsepower in this category. The completion of the Pearl Street Power Station in New York signaled the arrival of electricity as a public utility; the 200,000-horsepower capacity of industrial electricity—achieved almost totally in the 1890s—showed what was to come.

New and greater sources of power demanded materials either scarce or nonexistent at the close of the Civil War. Coal, for example, had familiarly appeared in stoves and hearths for generations. By 1900, however, it was being demanded not only as a source of domestic heat, but as raw material for coke essential to the manufacture of steel, as fuel for the giant coal-burning locomotives which had replaced the small wood-burners, and as a source of steam power used to generate electricity. In 1870 America produced about 33,000,000 tons of coal; in 1900 this output had been increased eightfold. Petroleum, too, was far from unknown

An advertisement by an oil well supply company dramatized visually the advance in drilling techniques. (Lithograph by Field-Beattie, 1891)

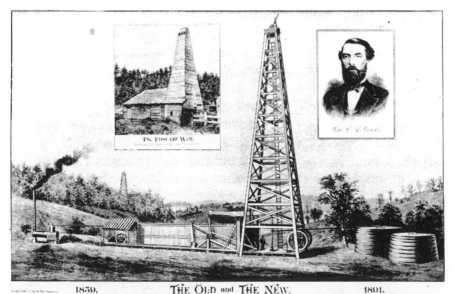

THE FIRST OIL WELL, HEIGHT OF DERRICK 34 FEET.   MODERN OIL WELL, HEIGHT OF DERRICK 82 FEET.

The awesome scale of a new steel-based heavy industry was captured by W. A. Rogers in this drawing reproduced in *Harper's Weekly*, March 14, 1891.

in 1865. But it was the discovery of great oil fields, the development of new refining techniques, and the organization of marketing empires that made possible the automobile age which was to follow. Even before 1900, petroleum products had changed the lives of Americans by serving as a lubricant for heavy machinery and by lighting millions of homes with kerosene and with petroleum gases which could be piped into the home rather than stored in bulk.

But the product most essential to the Age of Enterprise was steel. Much of the machinery which produced the prodigious power supply and replaced so many human arms and backs in 1900 would have been entirely conceivable generations earlier had the material to construct them been available. In fact a modern machinist might be astounded to see how far his ancestors had progressed toward machine manufacture with the use of wood and cast iron. But these materials were brittle; they fatigued easily; they were hard to make to the precise specifications required for advanced technology. The first dramatic answer to these problems came with the nearly simultaneous development in England and America of the Kelly-Bessemer process, which heated iron ore together with coke (coal from which impurities had been removed by prior burning) and applied to this mixture forced drafts of air at the right time, in the right place, and in the right proportions. The process was a delicate one. It required high grades of coal and iron to begin with, and the hand of a master foreman in the process.

Bringing Bessemer steel into production in commercial quantities provided one of the great sagas of the Age of Enterprise. It needed the discovery of the great Mesabi iron deposits in Minnesota. It needed the high-quality anthracite coal resources of western Pennsylvania. It needed a transportation revolution in the form of heavy-duty railroads, ore boats, carriers and cranes in order to assemble the weighty raw materials. It needed the metallurgical expertness of a new generation. It needed the organizational genius of a man like Andrew Carnegie.

All these ingredients were eventually supplied, and by 1867 Bessemer steel in small quantities was being used commercially in the United States. By the middle of the 1870s, American steel had entered the world market in the form of saws, shovels, frames, and locomotives. The rails for these locomotives could now be made in longer segments and joined more smoothly. Made of steel, they would last twenty years instead of wearing out after three years as iron rails did. Steel-wire nails could replace iron nails and outdo them in price and utility. Barbed wire would cut fencing costs in half and solve crucial problems for the plains farmer. The tin-plating of steel, fostered in the United States by the protective tariff in 1890, finally produced the domestic answer for a material in which to package and preserve foods. As a result, tinned or "canned" goods began to make the marketing and preparation of food more simple and varied than had ever been dreamed possible in the days of jars and barrels.

Eventually open-hearth techniques produced a steel that was tougher and more malleable than the products of the blast furnace; crucible steel remained essential for the manufacture of tools with cutting edges. The age of metallurgy had only begun. In its early stages it not only made possible the revolution in transportation, communications, manufacturing and power-production that changed the homes, stores and workshops of America, but it left behind its own folklore and glamour.

The manufacture of steel was a spectacular process. The ovens dwarfed in size most man-made objects that Victorian Americans had ever seen. The heat required to produce the steel created a climate suggestive of the hellish scenes depicted by the fire-and-brimstone preachers of the traveling circuit. As the air drafts were applied, enormous showers of sparks mounted to the sky, belittling any Fourth-of-July display. As a visual climax, the molten steel came tumbling out, shimmering in volcanic intensity and distorting the very air about it. In the midst of this elemental display, mysteriously goggled, his sinewy strength exaggerated by the gleam of heat-reflected sweat, moved the steelworker.

Captivated by the glamour of this work, and at the same time depressed by its limitations, the Slavs who migrated to the Monongahela Valley to become the nucleus of America's first generation of steelworkers created their startling version of the new folk hero of the industrial age. Materializing one Sunday at a local contest of strength, this seven-foot "Hunkie," with a back as broad as a door, easily lifted in one hand an 800-pound bar and won as his prize the valley's belle. For marriage, however, he had no time; all he needed was five good meals a day. His home was the mill where he worked night and day, feeding the open-hearth furnace, stirring the molten steel with his fingers and shaping rails with his bare hands. Who was he? His name was Magarac, a word meaning jackass. He was born inside a mountain and came to town in an ore train, he said, and he took off his shirt to substantiate his story:

> By Gods, he no tell lie. He was steelmans all right: all over he was steel same lak is from open hearth, steel hands, steel body, steel everything.

Although he had the prodigious strength of earlier folk heroes—Paul Bunyan of the lumbermen, Mike Fink of the riverboatmen—Joe Magarac was no free spirit who roamed the country with giant strides or strokes. He was more like John Henry, originally a West Virginia tunnel-driller, who died competing with the new machines. For Joe was well named for a beast of burden: he was a slave to his job, and he glamourized not so much man's power as man's subservience to a process and a product. When Joe Magarac died it was out of impatience with a mill owner who closed down Joe's furnace; without his work Joe was nothing. He deliberately melted himself into the first batch of steel from the relit furnace, and instructed the boss to build from this Magarac steel the finest new mill in the world—a mill that would never have to be shut down. And after they poured and rolled and cut that steel, they saw that it was the best steel ever made.

With new power and new materials Americans changed their world in myriad ways, but none more dramatically than the way in which they could talk and move across the surface of the earth. As the era opened, the power of an earlier invention, the telegraph, was demonstrated by the use the North made of it during the Civil War. President Abraham Lincoln and his Cabinet received prompt news of campaigns directly from the field, and strategy was put into rapid effect by use of the telegraph. At the end of the war there were 76,000 miles of telegraph lines in the United States; principally by following the railroads, the telegraph had spanned America and by 1900 had grown to a network of nearly 1,000,000 miles handling 63,000,000 messages a year.

The glamour of the telegraph wire was highlighted not only by its use in wartime but also by the spectacular efforts to submerge it beneath the Atlantic. This was done for the first time in 1858, and provoked prophecies of great consequences. Before the year was out, however, the signals began to fade and, mysteriously, cease altogether. It was not until 1866 that a new cable was laid and transatlantic communication successfully reestablished. Public exuberance over the second cable was caught by a Pennsylvania poet who likened Cyrus Field to Christopher Columbus, speaking metaphorically of the road the cable created "through Ocean's gloomy caves," and shouting:

> And o'er this turnpike Morse's steeds shall leap;
> Mermaids shall hear the lightening stage-whip crack—
> Ho, Neptune! make your loafers clear the track!

The great Exposition at Philadelphia was a cultural landmark for many reasons—its influence on taste, its insistent comparisons of 1876 with 1776—but particularly for its magnificent and hypnotic display of technology on the march. See page 71. (Lithograph by A. L. Weise, 1876)

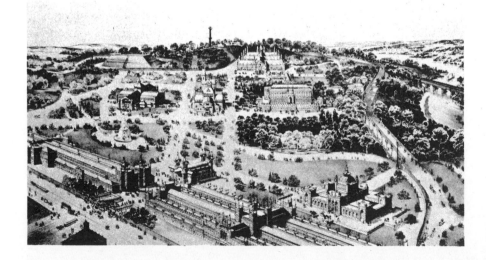

To many the telegraph and the Atlantic cable formed the central achievements of the Century of Progress, celebrated in 1876.

While the applause was going elsewhere, a display that arrived late at this 1876 Philadelphia Centennial Exposition and was tucked into an obscure corner of the Education Building, was readying an even greater impact. This impact might have been considerably delayed had it not been for the presence of a foreign visitor at that fair who had a good memory and an uncanny sense of timing. The visitor was Don Pedro, young Emperor of Brazil. His memory told him of an Alexander Bell whose teaching of deaf-mutes had so impressed him on an earlier visit to Boston. His timing brought him to Bell's display just as the Exposition's committee of judges had passed by with only the mildest sort of curiosity. Don Pedro, however, insisted on a demonstration from the man he had remembered. Bell obligingly walked to the other end of the line and spoke while Don Pedro held the receiver. "My God—it talks!" shouted the Emperor. Soon a crowd had gathered; the judges retraced their steps. Joseph Henry, America's pioneer electrical engineer, and Lord Kelvin of England both listened to the telephone and told the judges that they had just witnessed the greatest marvel of electrical science. Between the Brazilian Emperor's exclamation and public acceptance of the telephone lay a twisting and often discouraging road for Alexander Graham Bell and his associates. Yet by 1900 there were 1,500,000 telephones in America echoing that first utilitarian message carried by Bell's instrument: "Watson, come here; I want you." Granted in 1876, the telephone patent became the most valuable in terms of ultimate revenue ever issued by the patent office.

Equally important in modernizing communications was the typewriter, a device with many ancestors, including machines used in connection with telegraphy. But the modern typewriter owed its development to C. Latham Sholes, a

Milwaukee printer and editor. He combined ideas initiated by others and, through constant revision and experimentation, produced in the 1870s a machine which included the keyboard arrangement, the upstrike type bar, and the moving cylindrical platen. If Sholes was the typewriter's architect, it was the famous author and humorist, Mark Twain, who became its publicist. He liked the machine, he said, because it "piled an awful stack of words on one page" and because he could use it leaning back comfortably in his chair rather than hunched over a writing desk. *The Adventures of Tom Sawyer* became the first typewritten manuscirpt to go to the printers, leaving room for the wish that this machine had performed as well for the other novelists who subsequently used it. By 1900 it had become clear how profoundly this mechanical writer was to affect office procedures in commerce and government as well as the general facility and clarity of communication in all aspects of life.

The typewriter, the telephone and the telegraph were important for more than technological reasons; they played a unique part in the liberation of the American woman. At midcentury the only alternatives to marriage for a woman without the means and intelligence to pursue a profession were the endless drudgery of factory work or the demeaning and underpaid career of a shopgirl. As soon as employers discovered how efficiently women could manipulate switchboard plugs and typewriter keys, however, there arose a demand for office girls strong enough to overcome the Victorian prejudice against mingling the sexes in a place of business. With shorter hours, higher pay, and less physical exertion, the office girl was able to contemplate a career as a pleasant alternative to an unattractive marriage; thus, in the 1890s women telegraph and telephone operators increased 167 percent, and stenographers and typists 305 percent. Economically liberated by this technological opportunity, women looked confidently toward political and social equality.

Careers for women in the office, created by the typewriter and the telephone, freed them from the drudgery of factory labor or piece work but subjected them to other kinds of pressures and prejudices. (Photograph by Strohmeyer & Wyman, 1899)

The years before the Civil War had witnessed the introduction of steam-powered water transportation, the spread of an extensive network of canals, and the advance in design of the river steamboat and of the ocean-going steamship. Steam-powered ironclad vessels, the *Monitor* and the *Merrimac,* fought one of the best-remembered engagements of the Civil War. The novelty and the excitement of the water age—the keelboats of the legendary Mike Fink, the floating palaces etched indelibly on America's memory in Mark Twain's *Life on the Mississippi*—were symptomatic of an era already fading. As the railroads spread, the proportional importance of water transportation declined. Most of the canal systems soon ceased to function. Tonnage of freight carried on barges and canal boats fell drastically in the mid-1870s, and many communities never really regained the importance they had once owed to their position on the banks of a river or at the terminus of a canal. But with the continuing improvement of steamboats, the importance of barge traffic on the internal rivers began to mount once more, and has steadily if not spectacularly increased almost every year since the mid-1880s. Sometimes railroads incorporated riverboats into their passenger system; but, whether or not one were taking a boat as part of a train trip, it was still quite possible to travel in a luxurious if leisurely manner on America's major rivers throughout the Age of Enterprise.

The heralds of the automotive age were not, strangely, the sputterings of internal combustion engines, but the swish of bicycle tires and the groans of fallen riders whose high wheels had refused to remain upright in the deep ruts of a mud road. The bicycle in America has become more a part of young people's recreation than a functional vehicle for adults as it is in many parts of the world. But in the Age of Enterprise it was more than a toy or a way of getting to work: it was a craze. Bicycles of all shapes, sizes, and colors were suddenly everywhere. People wrote poems and songs to

In fluted columns and hand-carved panels the palatial luxury of river steamers penetrated even the "People's Evening Line." (Lithograph by Currier & Ives, 1878)

These early "high-wheelers" on rutted country roads demanded daring and skill. The tricycle in the foreground, with its off-center front wheel, protected the lady's modesty as well as her stability. (Aquarelle print by L. Prang after a watercolor by Hy Sandham, 1887)

them, spent weekends peddling them, changed the cut of their clothes to be more comfortable on them. The bicycle race—pitting first the old high-wheelers and later the safety bikes—furnished a major spectacle of the day. But the lasting importance of the bicycle arose not from its modishness but from its impulse toward still another form of transportation. Many of the bicycle manufacturers and repairmen —like George M. Pierce, who built the Pierce-Arrow— joined the ranks of the pioneers of the automobile industry. Even more important, perhaps, were the pressures exerted for good roads by the League of American Wheelmen and similar organizations. Before an automobile age could arrive, a highway had to become something better than a pair of ruts where horses had pulled farmers' wagons for a number of years. If the bicycle faddists had not paved the way, the motorists of the next age would have waited a lot longer for suitable surfaces on which to drive their runabouts.

Everyday life in America was not seriously affected by the automobile prior to 1900; but the groundwork had been laid for the great invasion of the horseless carriage which was to dominate the early years of the next century. European manufacturers had begun the regular production of cars while Americans were still innocently tinkering in their wheel and carriage shops, yet by 1900 Americans had largely caught up. A decision for the future had been made in favor of the gasoline-powered internal-combustion engine rather than steam or electric motors, and the oil refineries had produced a readily available fuel. The machine-tool industry had advanced to the point where it could accommodate the needs of automobile manufacture, including precision-made interchangeable parts. Some enterprising pioneers, like Alexander Winton of Cleveland, had even come to think in terms of a network of service stations to keep his cars running. The first automobile show and the founding of *Automobile Magazine,* both in 1900, fittingly signaled not only the beginning of a new century but also the dawn of a new transportation age. In 1900 there were 8,000 automobiles registered in the United States.

If the late nineteenth century is to be named for any aspect of its technology, there is not a doubt in the world that it should be called the railroad age. Henry Adams commented from a platform of informed bitterness that the age was mortgaged to the railroad; a less well-known writer, Edward Farquhar, echoing the thoughts of many of his more famous colleagues, hailed the locomotive as follows:

> O brazen monster bellowing by
> Art thou indeed our century?

Such statements as these hardly exaggerate the extent to which the railroad formed a center of interest and a dominating influence on the citizens of this era.

To understand this phenomenon one must begin with the

spectacular facts of railroad growth. Thirty-five thousand miles of road in 1865 had increased more than sevenfold by 1900. The continent had been spanned. On May 10, 1869, when the last spikes joined the Union Pacific and the Central Pacific in Promontory Point, Utah, there was not simply a local spilling of champagne with a group of amazed Indians in the background. It was a national holiday. The Liberty Bell was tolled. Parades, prayers, poems and thanksgiving services marked the day throughout the land. Orators proclaimed not only the liberation of the plains from Indian domination but the true establishment of the road to the wealth of the Indies and the unarguable meeting of East and West. By 1884, the Northern Pacific, Southern Pacific, and Sante Fe had all completed transcontinental routes. By 1900 the nation's railroads were reporting 16,000,000,000 passenger miles and $323,000,000 revenue. The railroad had not only attracted the major credit for leading civilization across the continent, but had plunged the country into an age of big business as well.

In the era between the age of waterways and the age of highways, the location of the railway was often a matter of life or death to an individual farmer or to an entire commu-

Frightening the Indians and scattering the buffalo, the railroad brought prosperity and civilization across the continent. This allegorical rendering shows how these facts loomed larger than words to the citizens of the "Railroad Age." (Lithograph by Currier & Ives, 1868)

THE GREAT RACE FOR THE WESTERN STAKES *1870*

Although Americans took a fascinated delight in the power struggles of the great railway tycoons, the outcome of iron-horse races like this one had serious consequences for all who depended on a particular right-of-way for their commercial livelihood. (Lithograph by Currier & Ives, 1860)

nity. Major public-relations campaigns were conducted to attract railroads, and by the railroads, in turn, to attract settlers and communities along their right of way. In the late 1860s, Commodore Vanderbilt fought a complicated war with "Uncle" Daniel Drew for favored access to the markets of New York City. Stocks were bought, cornered, inflated, secretly owned, traded and merged. Subsidies were swallowed voraciously wherever granted. Later Vanderbilt, with tacit control of the "Big Four" railroad serving Chicago, Cincinnati, Cleveland and St. Louis, fought for control of the Midwestern states with Jim Fisk's Erie Railroad and others. Alert states such as Pennsylvania offered prized subsidies for the completion of necessary roads, but also placed companies in competition with each other by setting deadlines and inviting road-laying races. On the other hand a city such as Cincinnati, a natural center for North-South trade in the water age, began to lose its commercial prominence because of the forbidding topography that discouraged railroads from approaching the city from the south. Its answer lay in the purchase of right of way, the construction of difficult bridges and railbeds, and the completion of a municipal railway stretching southward into Tennessee. The city's purpose was achieved when the road was leased permanently to the Southern Railway as part of a system which restored the city to something of the position it had held when river traffic dominated.

Railroads were the key to the commercial shape of the American future. Where they offered freight and passenger service at reasonable rates, they tended to bring prosperity and prominence. They also brought technology. The locomotive itself was the most widely used and one of the most efficient utilizations of steam power. Its parts and its rails required and encouraged the development of a modern steel industry. Laying rails taught Americans most of what they learned in the late nineteenth century about grading, banking, tunneling, and bridging. The air brake made possible the large trucks and buses of the twentieth century. Tank cars, coal cars, gondolas, and refrigerator cars produced the accumulation and distribution of goods necessary for the conduct of the industrial revolution.

Of course the railroads also brought problems. The "Great Strike" of 1877 was essentially a strike of trainmen; the famous Pullman Strike of 1894 occurred in the plant which manufactured passenger cars and was called by the American Railway Union. Farmers protested that the railroads were victimizing them by the fees they charged for storing and hauling their produce. The competitors of Standard Oil complained that a practice of rebates, or refunds given back to Standard Oil in consideration of their volume of business, made it impossible for smaller refineries to compete. None of these problems was really solved until it had been demonstrated that the railroads were, in effect, public utilities, and that the government had the right and duty to regulate their rates and practices as well as the wages and hours of their employees. The Interstate Commerce Act of 1887, the Sherman Anti-Trust Act of 1890, and the "Granger Cases" redressing rural grievances represented steps toward this realization.

The impact of the railroad was not only a matter of politics and economics; it was also a matter of sights and sounds. Even by the end of the Civil War the locomotive had ceased to resemble a tinkerer's toy, built of a barrel and a box set on a carriage frame. Most of the engines then in service rested on two pairs of large drive wheels located under the boiler and the cab, with two pairs of smaller wheels supporting and guiding the forward part of the boiler and "cow-catcher." The most prominent feature was the smokestack, shaped like a funnel, which sometimes changed its mind halfway up and either became a cylinder or tapered down to control the flow of smoke and propel it out of the path of the engineer's vision. This engine was made of cast iron and wood and towed in its wake a square tender stacked with cut and split logs. In the Far West, where wood was more plentiful than coal, logs served as locomotive fuel throughout the century; but in the rest of the country the tender became a coal car, and the fireman began picking up a shovel instead of a log. Answering a need for greater speed for passenger trains and greater power for freight trains, the locomotives steadily lengthened. By 1900 freight engines weighing 150 tons were being produced, some of them called "decapods" with as many as ten drive wheels. Made entirely of steel, riding on steel rails and built relatively close to the ground, the steam locomotive of the 1890s depicted the ultimate in brute power and rhythmic speed. Coupled to its impressively long tows, sometimes in tandem, the locomotive snorted impatiently on the siding. When fed its first jet of steam it spun its wheels with a chattering prediction of superabundant power. In motion its pistons and connecting arms spun a flashing visual symphony; its horizontal trails of steam and smoke exaggerated its impressive momentum. The rails sunk and clicked back into place as it passed over. The car couplings jangled. The swaying bell set up a metronomelike cadence against which contrasted the sounds of acceleration, and the powerful declaration of the steam whistle shattered unwary eardrums and set afire the imagination with thoughts of motion, adventure, and distant places.

For most Americans, the locomotive was the largest, noisiest, most powerful object they had ever seen. Few knew or cared what technology had made possible the steam giants of the road: the air brake, the automatic coupling, the link valve that cut off power at any point in the stroke, the block signal, the Vauclain system of compounding steam power, and the standard-gauge track. Everyone knew that the New York Central and the Pennsylvania were both making the New York-Chicago run in twenty-seven hours and that the famous old "999," the pride of the Chicago Fair of 1893, had surpassed 112 miles per hour on its run between Syracuse and Buffalo. Railroad news was front-page news, and going down to watch the train come in was as central and exciting a pastime in American communities as the steamboat arrival had been in an earlier age.

Americans not only took a factual interest in the railroad, they were hypnotized by it. Very quickly they adapted railroad phrases into their vocabulary. They got sidetracked or came uncoupled; or, if things were going better, they got up a full head of steam, highballed it, and warned their neighbors to clear the track. Expressing disapproval of almost anything, we exclaim even today, "That's a heck of a way to run a railroad!" Photographs of famous trains adorned the walls of dens and barns; colored lithographs of railroading scenes by Currier & Ives made their way into living rooms as well. Americans honored the railroad with architectural largesse; the most impressive building in town—whether it was built by the community or by the road—was very likely to be the depot. Nor was it long before the railroad achieved a special place in literature, song, and folklore. Poets as different as Emily Dickinson and Walt Whitman could not resist it. To the former the locomotive was a prodigious devourer of miles that could "step around a pile of mountains" and then come to rest, "docile and omnipotent." Whitman captured an even fuller range of the train's transcendent appeal to his contemporaries as he wrote of the locomotive's

> . . . measure'd dual throbbing and thy beat convulsive,
> Thy black cylindric body, golden brass and silvery steel,
> Thy ponderous side-bars, parallel and connecting rods,
>   gyrating, shuttling at thy sides,
> Thy metrical, now swelling pant and roar, now tapering
>   in the distance . . .
> Type of the modern—emblem of motion and power—
>   pulse of the continent . . .

The centrality of the railroad in American song and folk tale is obvious. From early tributes to those who built the roads, like John Henry and the singer of "I Been Working on the Railroad," to recent pop tunes like "Chattanooga Choochoo" and "The Atchison, Topeka, and the Santa Fe," the railroad has forever occupied our song. The man who claimed to have invented jazz, Jelly Roll Morton, said that the first blues he "no doubt heard in my life" began:

> 219 done took my baby away.
> 219 done took my babe away.
> 217 bring her back some day.

These numbers, of course, designated Southern Railway trains. The spotlight in train lore, shone brightest on the brave engineer, the unidentified man who steered Old '97 over the mighty rough road from Lynchburg to Danville, or

the six-foot-four-inch John Luther "Casey" Jones, who actually did drive for the Illinois Central between Memphis and
Canton. A man who knew him wrote, "In the early days of
railroading there was a real glamour to the rails. Into this
setting Casey, engineer of the Cannonball Express, fitted per-
fectly." The original Casey apparently possessed far more
substance than his pale shadow in song, who has somehow,
in most versions, been transferred to 'Frisco and left an un-
faithful widow in Salt Lake City. Wrote another of Casey's
fellow trainmen:

> I never saw him with his mouth closed—he always had
> a smile or a broad grin. The faster he could get his engine
> to roll, the happier he was. He would lean out of the cab
> window to watch his drivers, and when he got her going
> so fast that the side rods looked solid, he would look at
> you and grin all over, happy as a boy with his first pair
> of red boots. Yet he had a reputation as a safe engineer.
> With all his fast running I never knew of him piling them
> up, of any but a few derailments and never a rear-ender.
> He was either lucky, or else his judgment was as nearly
> perfect as human judgment can be.

Finishing his own run into Memphis on the wet Sunday of
April 29, 1900, Casey was told of a colleague's illness and
volunteered to drive an unfamiliar locomotive over the re-
verse run in spite of soggy embankments and a late start.
Having almost made up the lost time, and within twenty
miles of his destination, Casey had his first and last "rear-
ender." The original version of his song ends like this:

> 'Twas around this curve he saw a passenger train;
> Something happened in Casey's brain;
> Fireman jumped off, but Casey stayed on,
> He's a good engineer, but he's dead and gone—

Poor Casey was always all right,
He stuck to his post both day and night;
They loved to hear the whistle of old Number Three
As he came into Memphis on the old K.C. [I.C.?]

Headaches and heartaches and all kinds of pain
Are not apart from a railroad train;
Tales that are earnest, noble and gran'
Belong to the life of a railroad man.

Train wrecks were as hypnotic to Victorian Americans as the skill of the engineers and the speed of the locomotives. Minor folk heroes were made out of people like Kate Shelley of Moingona, Iowa, who bravely averted a train disaster; but more attention was paid to the scenes of gore resulting from caved-in trestles, loose tracks, faulty equipment or human error. The more famous wrecks were not only photographed but sketched, etched, lithographed, tinted and preserved with seemingly morbid curiosity. Rhymsters composed accompaniments for these scenes, memorializing the brave and unfortunate, or reveling in the carnage. Without some degree of danger it would have been impossible to arrive at the height

A natural fascination with disaster added a dimension of danger to the glamour of railroading at midcentury. See page 189. (Copyright John Collins, 1855)

R. F. Zogbaum's drawing, reproduced in the November 13, 1886, *Harper's Weekly*, showed some of the discomforts of transcontinental travel but invited the viewer to contrast this "ship of the plains" with its much more primitive predecessors.

of glamour and excitement enjoyed by railroading in those days.

Interest in trains was by no means confined to locomotives and disasters; Americans were, in fact, continuously fascinated by the startling evolution in passenger accommodations which took place during this era. For most passengers the train served as the quickest, cheapest, and—they hoped —the safest way of traveling between two points. The hard wooden benches were hardly inviting. Although coaches had been enclosed, their loose-fitting windows offered little protection against the soot and cinders of the road and against the vicissitudes of weather. Sleep was something passengers achieved with great determination: braced upright, jarred by the rough roadbeds that still predominated many lines, and often crowded by animals as well as fellow humans. Nourishment was brought along or else fought for at scandalous station restaurants during the hectic twenty-minute stop for meals. The trials of the meal stop were so universally ab-

Thomas Worth's cartoon exaggerated only slightly the problems of buying a meal on trains without dining cars. The original caption read "Five seconds for Refreshments." (Lithograph by Currier & Ives, 1884)

horred that they became a favorite subject for the embittered comedy of travel-wise cartoonists.

Before the end of the century, however, much of this had been changed. Coach seats were upholstered in leather, mohair, or caning. Vestibule platforms allowed passengers to pass from car to car without facing the unprotected blasts and jiggling hazards of the connecting platform. Steam heating and electric lighting replaced the discomfort and danger of the oil lamp and the wood stove. The changes which most captivated the public, however, were those introduced by George Pullman, a New York cabinetmaker, whose ride on an early sleeper set him to thinking how much better things could be. He devised an interior which was by day a comfortable lounge and by night became rows of beds with soft mattresses, warm blankets, and a measure of privacy. His crowning achievement was the "hotel car," which soon came to be called the diner. The contrast between the brutal sport of a twenty-minute dinner stop and the leisured luxury of fresh foods carefully prepared and served with vintage wines was dramatic indeed. When the sated passenger capped his ten-course meal with a stroll out onto the well-appointed observation platform at the rear of the train, clipped the end of his Havana cigar with a slender silver knife on the end of his watch chain, and inhaled carefully as he appraised the backward-rushing scenery, he felt himself on the very top of his railroad-minded world.

Actually the very top was reserved for the likes of J. P. Morgan, who commandeered whole trains when he traveled, reserving entire boxcars for racks of German wine. Only slightly lesser luminaries created public awe and resentment with the magnificence of their private cars, upholstered and enameled on every surface, tasseled and monogrammed with an excess of luxury reminiscent only of the palatial river-boats. This elaboration of railroad travel into something plush was lumped—sometimes sneeringly—by railroad men under the heading of "varnish." Most Americans seemed to admire and accept it. They patronized the varnish trains that made regular runs between large cities and the fashionable watering places of the era. They mirrored railroad tastes by filling their own sitting rooms with cane-back chairs and mohair upholstery. But there was also a good deal of resentment, particularly during hard times, when the passenger

George Pullman's answer to the "five-second meal stop" went to the opposite extreme in both luxury of furnishings and elegance of menu. Glimpses of wealthy passengers consuming wine and pheasant came to symbolize an indecent display of class differences. (Engraved after a drawing by Albert Bingham in *Frank Leslie's Illustrated Newspaper*, Janu-

train with its variety of accommodations became a symbol of class distinctions, when the railroad pass—especially in the hands of a Congressman or Senator—meant political corruption, and when the extravagances of the private cars contrasted with the needs of the many.

The truest index of the railroad's pervasiveness was its appearance in unlikely places. Its jargon had become part of everyday speech, and its power as metaphor had been tested by application to the broadest imaginable range of subjects. Many who argued the slavery question had made watchwords of the "slavery train" or the "freedom train"; after the war temperance crusaders favored railway metaphors. Drinking among passengers was a recognized travel hazard to those who found this practice objectionable, but the popularity of drinking away the miles was testified by one road which called itself "The Route of the Jug." Less easy to condone was drinking on the part of train crews, a reportedly common practice which led to some of the railway wrecks. Thus temperance literature was filled with references to smoking cars, drinking cars, and murder cars. Or one could read of a "gospel railway," built on rock, as opposed to "Satan's railway," laid, of course, on sand. If a writer claimed that he need no longer labor to the heights of creativity, but could simply take the next train up the mountain of the muses, he was surely joking; but what about the writer who called the locomotive "God's own trusty savior, helping to redeem mankind," or another who hailed it as a "genuine power that mocks the old bewailed divinity"? Were they serious? Whether this was humor or theology, it attested to the railroad's incredible penetration of the age's consciousness.

As this fascination with the railroad indicated, technological change was more than just a fact of American life. It was a matter of pride and preoccupation. It was, one might almost say, a center of worship. The great secular temples of this era were the international fairs: Paris in 1867, Vienna in

The penetration of the railroad into everyday life could be seen in this temperance allegory. Note how much more prominent was this new metaphor than such older ones as the "tree of life" and the "fires of hell." (Lithograph by Andrew B. Graham, 1894)

1873, Philadelphia in 1876, Paris again in 1878 and 1889, Melbourne in 1880 and 1888, Chicago in 1893, and Paris in 1900. What happened in these expositions, put most simply, was that American technology stole the show. Allowed grudging admission in cramped space at the fairs immediately following the Civil War, American inventors and manufacturers attracted so much applause and so many awards that each succeeding fair, regardless of its location, became more and more a display of American technology: machine tools, engines, farm equipment, sewing machines, typewriters, and later on electrical equipment, photographic and printing tools. The first chance Americans got to see their own progress on display was in the Centennial Exposition. Here Machinery Hall was not only centrally placed and grandly planned, but it became easily the most popular of the displays. In its center, overwhelming all else, stood the Corliss reciprocating steam engine in all its potent, gleaming magnificence, providing power for all the other displays in the hall. To those who saw it in 1876 it appeared to be an eighth wonder of the world, a final triumph of man over nature. According to contemporary accounts, Americans loved nothing better than to visit the fair, stare at and touch these new wonders. Curiosity on the part of the visitors was so insistent that one exhibitor, whose shingle machine had some dangerous features, hung a placard reading "Fingers cut off, free."

It was not only at fair time that Americans showed their love for machines. An event that combined science and technology, such as the opening of the Lick Observatory with its giant telescope, set off songs and celebrations all over the land. But the climax of the century for gadget-proud Americans came when the Westinghouse Company won the contract for lighting the World's Columbian Exposition in Chicago and turned it into a veritable electrical fair. With an enormous generator as a power source, with miles of wire

Promising to unlock the secrets of the heavens, the new telescope installed at Lick Observatory signaled another celebration of scientific and technological advance. (Lithograph by Morgan & Co., 1889)

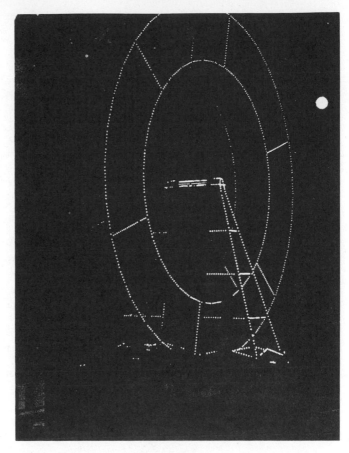

The ferris wheel at the Chicago fair. (Photograph by H. H. Bennett, 1893)

carrying the recently adopted alternating current and with variations of Edison's incandescent bulbs stuck in almost every corner, this fair assumed a nighttime aspect such as man had never seen. Its illuminated ferris wheel, another of the fair's innovations, dwarfed the full moon. Gazing at spectacles such as these, Americans at the end of the nineteenth century could compile endless lists of changes wrought by technology in their daily lives and could envisage a future wherein man's impressive control over nature would be extended even further.

Photograph by F. M. Steele about 1880.

3 Life on Farm and Frontier

As LATE AS 1900, farming was still America's major
enterprise, with a capital investment of $20,000,000,000,
a population representing more than half the nation, and
a two-thirds share in annual exports. In this enormous
enterprise, regional differences were much more important
than in commerce and manufacturing. Variations in climate,
soil and topography produced different crops and different
economic, political, and technological problems. The size,
extent, and fundamental diversity of agriculture made it less
susceptible to the kind of sweeping change that could be
projected by comparing photographs of Pittsburgh in 1865
and 1900. The typical farmer of 1900 had no telephone
poles along his front fence and no paving on his road to
town. The two innovations that were to change his life most
noticeably—electric power and the internal-combustion engine—had yet to arrive on the rural scene. Yet, looking
backward from the turn of the century, the farmer would

quickly recognize the different world he had come to inhabit since the close of the Civil War.

Farm families in 1865 were self-sufficient, isolated units spread out over much of the great face of North America, dependent on the cruelties and bounties of nature, and living in ways that differed little from the day when men first domesticated their flocks and harnessed the power of dray animals. For shelter the farm family might have anything from a tent to a plantation mansion, but its conveniences would scarcely be recognized as modern. A small, two-story frame house would have been average. Upstairs two unfinished rooms provided sleeping space for adults in one and children in the other. Downstairs two other rooms accommodated the family's wakeful functions. In the living room homemade furniture was grouped about a table on which a whale-oil or lard-oil lamp sputtered briefly after dark. The kitchen, with its greasy cast-iron sink and its monstrous wood-burning stove, housed the whole family on winter nights when bedroom temperatures invited frostbite.

As the years passed, those who had stayed on the farm and prospered would have made certain improvements. The house would be caulked and painted, the upstairs rooms plastered, and a first-floor addition leaned onto the original building to accommodate a parlor or dining room. A gallery, stretched between back door and barn, would keep the farmer dry as he came and went to milk and feed. A summer kitchen might be added to the existing outbuildings to keep the heat of the stove from adding to August discomforts, and an "earth closet," ancestor of the water closet, might be installed indoors to forestall freezing winter dashes to the outdoor privy. Some enterprising rural homeowners put in water and sewer pipes, but this proved a dangerous experiment for those who did not safeguard against contaminated water and waste-generated germs. A more usual answer to the bathing problem was an overhead tank in an outbuilding, which released a cold shower for summer bathers, and a washtub filled in front of the wood stove on winter Friday or Saturday nights.

On the living-room table a kerosene lamp would have replaced its cruder ancestor, and a coal stove added to the room's comfort. The housewife's busy needle would have provided curtains, runners, and cushions; a mail-order ad might have opened the door to a suite of manufactured furniture to replace the homemade chairs. The appearance of a piano, a sewing machine, or a hand-cranked wringer would have made a country wife feel truly blessed. In fact most farm families would have been proud to inhabit by 1900 the small-town home described in the opening chapter.

Farmhouses were not only smaller, but more crowded than their counterparts in town. Families with eight or ten children were considered to be more a rule than an exception in many parts of rural America, especially where exploding immigrant families swelled the totals. Nor were there any easy alternatives to keeping three generations under one roof when young couples and old folks were unable to provide independently.

For this rural multitude the day began before the dawn with chores for all: feeding animals, milking cows, chopping wood, and carrying water. When the housewife had lit her fire, fried ham and eggs, baked rolls and warmed what was left of last night's pie, she summoned to the table an eager band of trenchermen, appetites fully whetted by early-morning labors.

If it were planting or harvesting time, the breakfast would end with the exodus of the entire family from the board to the fields. Children would have been dismissed from school and the mother would be expected to bring along the very young, do her fair share of the seeding or cutting, leaving the fields only in time to prepare the heavy noontime dinner or only slightly lighter evening supper. Daughters, of course, were there to lighten their mother's load, and each female child made mother's drudgery a little less severe. It is hard to know whether to pity more the harrassed wife with a family of ten sons and no daughters, or the lonely plowman working to feed a completely female family.

Whatever their sex, the children of a farm family would be around the house much more than their town cousins. School terms did not begin until harvest was over and ended in time for spring planting. Many rural schools were of the kind made famous in Edward Eggleston's *The Hoosier Schoolmaster*. They contained only one room in which the distraught teacher divided his time between the many age levels represented. Girls made a practice of sitting on their feet to keep them warm in the inadequately heated shacks; local bullies made their reputations by threatening and sometimes thrashing the schoolmaster. Instruction was what might be expected from a profession that was scandalously underpaid and treated with a deference that matched the salary. It was not hard to understand why so many farm children stayed barely long enough to learn their "three Rs," or even why some of them mastered arithmetic and spelling only at home. By 1900, graded, consolidated schools had come to some areas; but for most rural Americans in the nineteenth century, education amounted only to three or four short years at the little old red schoolhouse.

Schools often dismissed at noon, and the whole family assembled for a hearty assortment of fresh produce from the kitchen garden or home-canned delicacies from the shelves. Potatoes, apples, milk, butter, eggs, and cured meats were stored in the springhouse and came to the table cool and inviting in summer. Unless the farm raised livestock for slaughter, the meat staple would have been salt pork, which appeared in a number of disguises through the long winter. Breads and pastries were expected with every meal, and farm women became proud and prolific bakers. Coffee and tea were luxury items, present only when finances were easy; but a coffee substitute made from roasted peas served at other times.

Following dinner the family returned to its labors. Young children were given such lighter tasks as feeding the chickens or hogs, gathering eggs, or weeding the vegetable garden. A boy of twelve, however, was considered ready to do a man's work and proudly took his place behind the plow, hoping the straightness of his furrows would match those of his dad. When the women were not needed in the fields, they had plenty to keep them busy indoors. Farm families in many areas continued to depend on homemade clothes long after city dwellers had turned to factory-made products. Sometimes bolts of cloth were brought home from the general store; but Hamlin Garland, whose pen made famous rural life on the "middle border," remembered his mother weaving cotton cloth to make sheets, bedspreads, shirts, and dresses. Sewing was more than utilitarian; mother and daughters worked with pride on their quilts, samplers, and trousseaus.

Supper was only slightly less formidable than dinner. It was served about five o'clock in winter, but in spring and fall it often had to wait until the field workers had used up the daylight. Evenings in a farmhouse were not markedly different from those in a village home of the 1860s, but they were shorter and more predictably confined to the family. Gathered around a lamplit table, the youngsters might practice addition or spelling while the women continued to ply their needles. Daily Bible reading was likely; next in popularity were the mail-order catalogs and the publications of the Grange and Farmers' Institutes. Cards, parlor games, stereopticons, and music all found their place in the evening programs; but, tired by a day of physical labor and anticipating a predawn rising, the farm family promptly followed the sun to bed.

Even more strictly than his village neighbors, the farmer kept an old-fashioned Sabbath with church services lasting most of the day, very little else was deemed proper on the Lord's Day. Saturday, however, offered an active change from the repetitive round of agricultural chores. Up with the sun as usual, mother fixed a breakfast, packed a lunch, made the children presentable and dressed herself in a starched cotton dress and bonnet. Father hitched the team to the wagon, loaded it with produce for market and a gap-toothed harrow, the repair of which had proved beyond his own smithing skills. Mother was helped onto the seat and, while the children struggled for a comfortable place on top of the load, father swung the team out into the dusty, rutted road and headed for town. Once there he would find dozens of farm families like his own, climbing down from wagon seats or, if they had no freight to haul, stepping out of spring buggies. Each family had its habitual spot around the village green or in front of the drugstore where the horses were hitched; and, even before they had alighted from their vehicles, they were already engaged in eager conversation with their neighbors.

After a week of self-contained family life, the sound of other voices was as welcome as the rustle of a gentle July shower on a parched cornfield. Children left off fighting with their brothers and sisters and sought out friends their own age, perhaps drifting over to the schoolyard to join a game of baseball, hopscotch, or crack-the-whip. Mothers gathered their older daughters around them and marched determinedly for the yard-goods counter of the general store, where they scored the clerk for his lack of an adequate selection and his unreasonable prices, and finally bought a dozen yards of the first bolt they had examined. Father's first stop

The Saturday migration to town was captured in this photograph by W. H. McQuiston near the end of the century. The predominance of spring buggies over wagons shows this to have been a prosperous farm county.

was likely to be the harnessmaker's or blacksmith's, where he left a horse to be shod or a piece of equipment to be repaired. Next he went to the feed-and-grain dealer to arrange for storage, marketing, and credit. Before long, however, he would find himself joining his fellow farmers around the pot-bellied stove or against the porch rail at the general store.

The general store, especially in the days before daily mail, telephone, and good roads, formed the nexus of rural communication. Men had to come there in order to purchase staples and to arrange credit against the next harvest. They enjoyed the appetizing aromas rising from the barrels of pickles and the rows of smoked meats. It was tempting to linger in this atmosphere and to mix with it the aroma of their tobacco and the pungency of their words. Having exhausted the weather, they would turn to other topics of common interest: the latest feeds and fertilizers; new theories of crop rotation; business news about the fluctuating price of grains in various markets; political problems concerning the sale of land, the regulation of railroads, and federal fiscal policies. These conversations sometimes had immediate consequences; for example, the loan of an animal for breeding purposes. Equally important were the long-range consequences that took the shape of rural organizations dedicated to serving the farmer socially, economically, and politically. The seeds for this organized change were sown in those informal Saturday afternoons at the general store which made up America's rural parliament.

Saturdays had their grim moments when the children were introduced to the not-so-painless dental chairs of the period. This was also the day for consulting the doctor about that swollen elbow which would not subside; but if the patient survived the bumpy wagon ride into town, he was probably in condition to withstand whatever the local doctor could do to him. With box lunches eaten, shopping done, and mended tools retrieved, the family reassembled and, amid farewell cries of "See you next week," got ready to bounce along home by sunset.

Then, as ever, variations in rural routines came more with the seasons' changes than with the days of the week. In the home this meant spring cleaning, less arduous in the smaller and more simply furnished farmhouse, but prolonged by the necessity of cleaning the barn and the other outbuildings which had stagnated over the winter months. As for the fall canning season, it was a much more serious process on the farm where home-preserved foods substituted for daily access to a grocery. Some chores meant social occasions, as when whole communities would assemble for a husking or quilting bee. Monotonous work went faster in groups where prizes were given for speed and dexterity, and where music and refreshments made work light. Particularly in newly settled communities, where there were roofs to be raised and fences to be strung, did families gather with a frequency and joy that became the envy of their children, who followed more settled and independent routines.

The completion of a barn was celebrated by an indigenous custom which came to be known as the barn dance. According to Thomas D. Clark, historian of the Southern frontier,

When H. W. Pierce copyrighted this photograph of a drawing in 1876, quilting bees were already old-fashioned in many urban neighborhoods. Occasions combining work and socializing remained prominent in rural life well past the turn of the century.

More social than functional was the husking party, where finding a red ear gave a man the right to kiss the girl of his choice—if he could catch her. (Wood engraving in *Ballou's Pictorial Drawing-Room Companion,* November 28, 1857)

this rite was originally called, a "bran dance," named for the husks that were thrown on the rough floor. The rigors of the dance were supposed to smooth and polish the unplaned boards. Whether the dance took place in a newly finished barn or as part of the church social, it was a great event in many parts of the country. Hamlin Garland described the gleeful anticipation as the fiddler-caller placed his chair on top of a kitchen table, tuned his strings, waved his bow with a "Lively now!" and positioned the couples. Then, with a mighty clump from his size-fourteen boot, and the chant of "Honors *tew* your pardners—right and left Four," the dance was on. Cider and cold meats, apples and pastries filled the hungry throats at intermission as these hardworking folk exuberantly expressed their satisfaction at a job completed. On into the night went the schottische-like rhythms, the scrapings of the bow to "Turkey in the Straw" and "Money

Musk," and the all-but-unintelligible instructions of the
caller to "al-le-man' left" or "promenade right." One of the
popular tunes was the folk song "Old Dan Tucker." At a
certain point the fiddler would shout "Go in Tucker!"
whereat a single man could claim any temporarily unat-
tached girl. Thus began one version of the ballroom custom
of "cutting in."

With his city cousins the farmer shared many holidays:
Thanksgiving, Christmas, and Easter. Like the small-town
family of the 1860s, the farm family kept pretty much to
itself on such occasions, including only close relatives in the
principal festivities and making church-going a major feature. The great social events on the farmer's calendar came
in the summer, and he celebrated them as predictably with a
picnic as the city dweller did with a parade. The Fourth of
July was the great picnic, and families would travel many
miles to spread their baskets within earshot of a famous spell-
binder. A resident of Marion, Kansas, a small agricultural
community, had this to record in his diary for July 4, 1887:

> Marion had a big time today. "John Dewitt Miller" spoke
> and made a fine speech. Hattie, Lizzie and I attended a

The speaker at this Fourth of July picnic had lost the attention of
his audience and was being mimicked by the boy perched on the
refreshment stand. On most such occasions the old and new "Old
Glories" were waved with greater effect. (Engraving after drawing
by Charles G. Bush, *Harper's Weekly*, July 6, 1867)

baseball game between our boys and Florence. We won, of course. The display of fireworks fired from the schoolhouse on the hill was very nice.

Throughout the rest of the summer church picnics, lodge picnics, temperance-society picnics, and Grange picnics polished the art of outdoor eating. To mention picnic to a Gilded Age family was not to suggest a peanut-butter sandwich, a bag of potato chips, and a carton of soft drinks. Here, for example, is the menu of one such outing held in Wisconsin in 1890:

English rolls	Coconut cake
Whole-wheat bread	Ribbon cake
Ham sandwiches	Pound cake
Veal loaf	Consistent American pie
Sliced tongue	Fruit
Meats	Tropical bananas
Watercress	Old Government Java
Cream cheese	Sugar cubes
Jell à la fruit	Jersey cream

Ice water

Picnics were more than sharing food with the ants and listening to orations. They included swimming and boating whenever possible, games and races, and always a few songs toward twilight.

Two outings were likely to tempt a farm family farthest off the beaten path: the county fair and the circus. Rural fairs are almost as old as farms; but Elkanah Watson's early-nineteenth-century American version was intended to be a rather serious conclave at which could be tested and discussed the merits of breeding, feeding, and fertilization. After the close of the Civil War thousands of state and county agricultural societies began to follow Watson's example by holding fairs with this serious purpose in mind. Soon, however, many amusement and competitive features were added, and the

Exhibitions of new equipment, prize produce and livestock mixed with balloon ascensions and harness races to make county fairs a stellar summer attraction. (Lithograph by Currier & Ives, 1894)

great state fairs of the 1890s attracted tens of thousands of visitors. For most farmers the fair meant a one-day trip to the county seat where the family could display its finest horses and hogs, melons and preserves. Association judges awarded prizes for the ladies' best cakes and jams and to the winners of the plowing and shucking contests. To be the first up the greased pole, to collapse short of the sack-race finish line, or to catch it in the face in the egg-throwing contest—these were episodes that could be relived all winter. To these picnic games the larger fairs added balloon ascensions, bicycle tournaments, football and baseball contests; but the biggest attraction was unfailingly the horse race. Men and boys raced their own nags at first, either from crude sulkies or from the saddle. Gradually the tracks improved, the bicycle sulky was developed, and a class of professional racers were touring the fairs and making commonplace the fabulous 2:08:45-minute mile run by "Maud S" in the 1870s.

As the fairs began to attract sideshows, pitchmen, barkers, and freak shows, they came more and more to resemble the traveling circuses enormously popular throughout America in this heyday of the big top, but especially important to the farmer. To the young Hamlin Garland the circus came "trailing clouds of glorified dust and filling our minds with the color of romance. . . . It brought to our ears the latest band pieces and taught us the popular songs. It furnished us with jokes. It relieved our dullness. It gave us something to talk about." The biggest circuses—those of William C. Coup, James A. Bailey, and P. T. Barnum—never got to the small towns; but somehow the farmers managed to get either to the city for "The Greatest Show on Earth," or to a smaller town for some lesser version which made no less extravagant claims. Miles Orton's New York and New Orleans Circus, Menagerie and Wild West Show, which charged only twenty-five cents admission on its one-night stands throughout Illinois, did not have Barnum's great elephant Jumbo, bought from London's Royal Zoological Gardens at an enormous

Big shows like this one traveled by special train, performed under enormous tents, and began their pitch with carefully arranged parades. (Lithograph by Calvert Co., 1891)

BUFFALO BILLS WILD WEST

AND CONGRESS OF ROUGH RIDERS OF THE WORLD.

WILD RIVALRIES OF SAVAGE, BARBAROUS AND CIVILIZED RACES.

Sometimes following a circus act and sometimes traveling on their own, Wild West shows reenacted Indian battles, stirring the tanbark with enthusiastic displays of horsemanship and markmanship. Some troupes developed a stage version of the Battle of San Juan Hill to celebrate the Rough Riders' wartime triumph. (Lithograph by Courier, 1898)

price to English pride. It did have an advance crew of posterhangers ready to trade free tickets for the side of a prominent barn. It did have a steam calliope and a brass band that could straighten the backs of listening lads and imperil the show windows along the parade route. It did have a pair of work elephants who helped to move the cages and tighten the ropes as the big top went up.

The features of the circus—the birdlike trapeze athletes, the whip-cracking ringmaster, the trained animals—are little changed today and can be readily called to mind. What is hard to imagine is the excitement this spectacle incited in rural folk whose only other diversions were homemade. No wonder the coming of the circus quickened pulses weeks before its arrival. No wonder local boys fought for the privilege of watering the elephants and promised to run away with the troupe next year for sure. No wonder rural audiences could line the streets for the morning parade, visit sideshows all afternoon, and still be willing to stay after the main show for the Wild West or minstrel acts. They were literally soaking up enough entertainment that one day to last the other 364.

The routines of rural life, close to the natural essentials, were a matter of great joy to many who experienced them in this era. If the farmer or his forebears had been shrewd enough to settle on a fertile homestead with plentiful rainfall and convenient access to transportation, then life might indeed by pleasant as well as prosperous. The chance for rural prosperity depended mainly on two factors: region and race. In the Middle Atlantic states—New York, New Jersey, Pennsylvania—farmers prospered because of the steadily increasing markets created for their produce by the booming cities and by the network of roads and railroads that covered The East more thoroughly than other regions. The old Northwest Territory—Ohio, Indiana, Illinois, Michigan, Wisconsin, Minnesota—had its problems at the beginning of this era. But by 1900, abetted by technology and topography, it had adapted to a generally profitable specialized agriculture, concentrating on corn in the southern and eastern part of this region, wheat in the north and west, and dairy products in the central portions. The relative prosperity of this region afforded it the means of expression, and the Middle West therefore took a prominent part in the promotion of agricultural programs; the real problem areas were New England, the South, and the trans-Mississippi West.

The problem of New England was a natural one. The short growing season, the rocky soil, and the hilly terrain combined to eliminate any real chance for competitive marketing against the products of the flat and fertile Midwest. The Civil War, with its shortages, prolonged the need for New England produce, but soon transportation and technology were giving a decisive advantage to the Western farmer. In the South it was a question of beginning again without capital, without cash markets, and under the restraints and confusions of an occupation government. Although live-stock and farm equipment had been part of wartime losses, the South did almost miraculously rise again through the ingenuity of men like the father of James B. Duke, the tobacco tycoon, who traveled and bartered his way from starvation to survival, and through the sheer grit of former plantation belles who, in the absence of dray animals, har-nessed themselves to the battered plow. Two old errors, habitual indebtedness and overdependence on cotton, rose hand-in-hand with revived productivity to entrap the South-ern farmer as they had before the war. In the gradual diver-sification of the region through citrus, tobacco, and textile mills lay the only permanent solution.

Another problem remained unsolved and, for the most part, unnoticed: how the freed Negro was to fit into American life. Up to 1900 the main context of this problem was rural and Southern. Eight out of nine Negroes still lived in the greater South, most of them in the old plantation country, and nearly seven out of these eight lived on farms or in small towns. Sharecropping cotton for his old master, or for some-one like him, the Negro had gained the right to a family, a church, and some schooling—important gains, indeed—but not much else. His chances for economic advancement were slim, his chances for political expression nil. Many Negroes worked at nonfarming chores; some served their fellow Ne-groes in skilled capacities, but in the white world they ap-peared principally as domestics, launderers, janitors, porters, and bootblacks. With the withdrawal of Northern occupation troops and the end of the Reconstruction in 1877, the thrust of the Negro into positions of responsibility was reversed. The Southern Democratic party, and with it the concept of white leadership, was restored. Silence on racial questions became the order of the day. The Negro continued his life as a free citizen with very few assets, in an impoverished agri-cultural region, and as part of a culture which accepted him either as a dependent inferior or, at best, as a segregated equal. Everyday life for Negro Americans remained throughout this era predominantly a matter of primitive tenant farming or menial labor in small towns without much apparent hope of change for the better. Even the discovery of the sociological frontier on which the Negro lived remained for twentieth-century explorers.

The West shared many important characteristics with the South. It was constantly encouraged by the combination of high prices for local commodities and cheap or free land. Yet, like the South, it suffered from a general agricultural depression and struggled with the severe problem of a colored minority, the red man. At the close of the Civil War the enormous area between the Missouri and the Sierras contained 225,000 Indians, 400,000 white settlers, and at least 15,000,000 buffalo. By 1900 the Indians had been tamed and dispersed, the buffalo exterminated, and 1,500,000 white settlers were pursuing ways of life which demonstrated their conquest of the plains wilderness. This achievement was realized only at the cost of considerable misunderstanding, waste, hardship and violence.

The era opened with violence on the Indian front. In 1864 some Cheyennes attacked along Ben Holladay's stageline east of Denver; a troop of volunteers retaliated with the atrocious slaughter of 500 friendly Cheyenne and Arapaho, mostly women and children. Soon 25,000 United States troops were in the field against warring tribes from the Dakotas to New Mexico. From the Indian viewpoint, these outbreaks were inevitable. For centuries, tribes had been evicted from their chosen land and moved westward, now into distinctly undesirable areas. The hunters of the plain were being cut off from their livelihood: elk, deer, antelope, and buffalo. The Indian's dealings with the white man were muddied by a federal attitude so vascillating it could hardly be called a policy, and further complicated by conflicts between branches of the government: the missionary attitude of the

Indians, protecting land and game they considered rightfully theirs, made frontier life sporadically violent through the mid '70s. (Engraving in *Frank Leslie's Illustrated Newspaper*, May 17, 1873)

Interior Department as contrasted with the forceful approaches of the War Department. At times the Indian found himself dealing with people who made no bones about declaring that the only answer to the Indian problem was extermination.

The Indian, skilled at guerrilla warfare and master of the plains pony, resisted extinction so well that even General Sherman admitted that 30 Indians could tie up 3,000 soldiers. Through the 1860s and '70s, and sporadically into the '80s, Indians produced nightmares for stage and pony-express riders, for railroad constructions gangs, for cowboys and settlers in isolated territories, as well as for the troops themselves. But the battle was a losing one. General George Custer led 226 men into an ambush at the Little Big Horn in 1876, and the Indians won their last major victory in "Custer's Last Stand." The main federal force quickly retaliated, ending large-scale warfare in the North. The next year the Nez Percé of the Snake Valley were subdued by Colonel N. A. Miles, and only the celebrated Victorio and Geronimo of the Apaches were left to make sizable skirmishes.

As the Indian ceased to be a military threat, he also ceased to be the cause of concern for the white man. The novelist Helen Hunt Jackson attempted in *A Century of Dishonor* (1881) what Harriet Beecher Stowe had done for the Negro, commenting on the abuse and neglect to which the red man had been subjected. Her books gave impetus to the formation of Indian Rights Associations and helped pass the Dawes Act of 1887. To give the Indian an alternative to life on the reservation, this legislation offered full citizenship and a twenty-five year title to a 160-acre land grant. Although many took advantage of this opportunity to trade nomadic life for agriculture and assimilation, they were often discouraged by the poor quality of available land. Once again the Indian was offered only what the white man had not wanted. His choice lay between a subsidized idleness on the reservation, or a struggling existence on marginal farmland in a culture that did not accept him without qualifications. With the Negro, the Indian in 1900 awaited public recognition of his major problems.

On the Great Plains the white settler found not only thousands of Indians but also millions of buffaloes; for a while the enormous herds of bison formed a spectacular feature of his everyday life. Railroad builders had been hampered by migrating herds, but had also lived off them, as had the Indians. Buffalo meat, although strong for some tastes, is quite edible; and the hides, when properly cured, are serviceably warm and woolly like sheepskin. But the white settler chose to regard the buffalo as an unfriendly nuisance, rather than as a natural resource. The Union Pacific began the process of decimation by splitting the buffalo world into a northern herd and a southern herd. Each new road and major trail

Hunting buffalo was seldom as dramatic as here depicted. Unwanted remains of the great herds eventually littered the plains and brought the bison close to extinction. (Lithograph by Currier & Ives, 1871)

split the herds further. Meanwhile, the hunters were having a field day, as permanent open season was declared. The difficulty of the hunt can be judged by two facts: a normal party consisted of two skinners for every hunter, and the principal problem of the hunter was to keep his rifle from overheating as the result of continuous use. The meat was almost entirely wasted. For a while, the hides furnished a good living for enterprising hunters and tanners; but by 1875 the market had become so glutted that bull bisons' hides sold for only sixty-five cents. In the West they were used as rugs.

With the Indian and buffalo vanquished, the plains were opened up to a new kind of warfare: cattleman vs. farmer. At the end of the Civil War, when farming had got only as far west as the Missouri Valley, the Texas cattleman discovered the enormous natural pasture called the Great Plains. Because his commerce had been cut off during the war, he

Broad-hatted cowhands spent many lonely nights urging longhorned cattle northward to better grazing and, eventually, to the railheads and market. (Engraving after a sketch by A. R. Waud in *Harper's Weekly*, October 19, 1867)

now found himself overstocked with cattle and running short of his Texas rangeland. His solution was to join with his neighbors in driving huge herds northward onto the plains just being cleared of buffalo. Each spring the cowhands would round up the herd, brand and castrate the calves, doctor the diseased critters, and prepare for the long drive of the full-grown steers to the nearest railroad.

The cattle business had plenty of hardships. Herds could be stampeded or rustled and were prey for Indians as well as predatory animals. If they were not driven carefully and allowed plenty of pasturage along the way, they might arrive at the market skimpy and scrawny, and fattening them for market again would eat up all the potential profits. Caring for these often unpredictable critters produced a breed of men who have become the country's preeminent folk heroes. Garbed colorfully but functionally in a broad-brimmed hat and a bandana for protection against sun and rain, and in the buckskins and boots that would resist the friction of days on horseback, keep feet in stirrups, and filter most of the trail dirt, the cowboy sat in a weighty, hand-tooled saddle that was his pride as well as his home. His job, his life depended on the responsive quarterhorse that could answer the commands of his knee pressure while his hands were kept free for roping and, sometimes, shooting. At night he sang minor-keyed ballads which soothed restless cattle as they told of his own loneliness. "The Cowboy's Lament" ("Streets of Laredo"), "Bury Me Not on the Lone Prairie," "Get Along, Little Dogies." Three verses from "Trail to Mexico" represent the tone of these songs:

'Twas in the springtime of the year,
I volunteered to drive the steers,
I'll tell you boys, 'twas a long hard go,
As the trail rolled on into Mexico.

When I arrived in Mexico,
I wanted my girl but I could not go,
So I wrote a letter to my dear,
But not a word from her did I hear.

So I returned to my one time home,
Inquired for the girl whom I adore,
She said, "Young man, I've wed a richer life,
Therefore young fellow, go and get another wife.

Cowboys did not get rich, but their employers often did in spite of the many difficulties. As the railheads moved westward to Wichita and Dodge City, and the trail shortened, cattlemen prospered. A shrewd bargain at stockyard or railhead might easily double the year's investment, with nothing but a crude bunkhouse to maintain and free use of all the pasture one could want. Problems came with the settlers, who built fences across the trails, dammed up for irrigation the streams that cattle had used for watering, and even spoiled the open range by grazing sheep who chewed vegetation off so close to the roots that it would not grow back again. Furthermore, the farmers were changing the towns:

building churches and schools and promoting a family-centered law and order, which conflicted head on with the male world of the trailriders and their demands for strong drink, gay women, and unrestrained gambling at the trail's end.

The inevitable clash was bitter and prolonged. Ranchers made armies of their cowhands, cut down the settlers' fences, and shot their way to water, if necessary. As the farmers organized and sought legal protection, the cattlemen's associations fought legally by petitioning for water-rights legislation and illegally by threatening and killing their opposition. As late as 1892 in Wyoming's infamous Johnson County War, big cattlemen were still hiring guns to dispose of the small ranchers who got in their way. But time was on the side of the settlers; in the end the cattlemen were building their own fences and cooperating in promoting measures for the common Western good.

The farmer's problems were by no means confined to Indians, buffaloes, and cattlemen. As he left the great river valleys of the Middle West and moved beyond the ninety-eighth meridian, he came into country where his skills acquired in the East or in Europe were to fail him. He came primarily because of the cheap land. The Homestead Act, passed during the Civil War, offered quarter sections (160 acres) to any who would file on the land and improve it. During the first twenty years of the act's existence, nearly 500,000 petitions were filed. Railroads, granted enormous tracts as part of the federal subsidy to encourage transcontinental lines, began to sell this land at negligible prices in order to settle the right of way and increase traffic. An ax, a plow, a rifle, a mule, and a bag of seed was all that seemed needed in order to realize the dream of so many: a farm of their own. Full of hope, they loaded their possessions in a wagon, painted "Kansas or Bust" on the side, and set sail o'er the prairie sea. Not long after, many of these same families could have been seen heading back east, their motto now changed to: "In God We Trusted, in Kansas We Busted."

A sod house was considered a notable luxury in many parts of the treeless plains, especially when glazed and roofed like this one. (Photograph in the Wittemann Collection, 1882)

Things would start off well enough. The claim would be surveyed and filed. Hitching up the plow, the farmer would dig a furrow around his boundaries, creating what the law recognized as a fence. Viewing the seemingly endless and boundlessly fertile plains, the family might indeed think they had arrived in God's country. Trouble began when they looked for shelter, for the forests so abundant in the East were lacking here. Instead of cutting logs they might excavate living room underground and roof it over. These "dugouts" were, of course, impossible to clean and were famous for the centipedes and other vermin they attracted. One step above the dugout was the "soddy," a structure made by cutting turf into squares and using them as bricks. As a temporary shelter they were better than a tent, but hardly proof against the elements.

Other problems occurred as soon as a crop or livestock were contemplated. With no natural growth of timber, how

A terrifying hazard to beast and man, the prairie fire darkened the skies for days and left an ineradicable fear interwoven with the desolation it caused. (Lithograph by Currier & Ives, 1872)

could the land be fenced? The answer was eventually found in barbed wire; before this solution many hours were wasted chasing strays, and many unprotected crops destroyed. As the crop came up, new problems continued to emerge. There were rusts and blights attacking prairie grain that were unfamiliar in the East. Locusts, cinch bugs, and grasshoppers came in giant sizes, enormous numbers, and with bottomless appetites. The most spectacular hazard of all, the prairie fire, destroyed everything in its path and left an indelible impression on anyone who ever witnessed it. Martha L. Smith, whose Oklahoma Territory farmhouse was saved by helpful cowboys who started a backfire, complained of how long it took her to clean the burned grass out of everything. Never again, she shuddered to her diary, could she look out over the prairie without imagining she saw smoke.

There were two problems more basic than any of the others: aridity and distance. Covered with naturally fertile soil, the plains had been made to look their best by a few years of unnaturally abundant rainfall. But in the 1880s they began to revert to their usual state of semiaridity. The farmers thought they were being plagued by droughts; in fact they were encountering only the normal state of affairs in the High Plains. Eventually a bitter humor developed on this subject, producing the yarn about the plainsman who got hit by a drop of water and recovered only after several buckets of dirt were thrown in his face. Where there were mountains nearby, and runoff from the melted snow could be channeled for summer use, irrigation gave a ready solution. However in the Dakotas, in western Kansas and Nebraska, and in eastern Colorado, there appeared no easy answer. Where there was adequate subterranean water, windmills were eventually used to pump and irrigate. New kinds of seed and new planting techniques were introduced, resulting in the highly prosperous "bonanza" farms where golden grains eventually stretched across the enormous landholdings acquired from the "back-

The High Plains were blessed with fertile soil, but in normal years they required artificial irrigation to make them arable. Complicated sluiceways brought melting snows from the mountains and made farming profitable where altitude and latitude were not too extreme. (Engraving after drawings by Frenzeny and Tavernier in *Harper's Weekly*, June 20, 1874)

trailers" who had "busted," and where machines reaped fabulous harvests.

For the westward-moving migrant who cherished his "elbow room," distance was a highly valued asset of the plains. With distance, however, went isolation and loneliness. Practical problems raised by distance were real enough to the farmer, but the psychological problem of isolation was particularly wearing on his wife. With the nearest neighbor miles away, months could easily pass without a visit. When fire, Indians, sickness or other emergencies arose, the lack of help nearby could be fatal; and the perpetual threat of having to meet a crisis single-handed created an unhealthy state of mind. "Sweet Betsy from Pike," in the folk song, traveled west, fought off Indians, and homesteaded with greater vigor than her mate; but for most farm women of the prairie, including Hamlin Garland's mother, life was trying both for the backbreaking toil and for the unrelieved monotony imposed by distance. Out on the deserted plains, wrote one poet, grease wood and salt sage are the only living things; men and women are small and futile: "lonelier than God."

Each region had its unique blend of promise and problems, but to rural America as a whole things looked dim. Farmers everywhere resented the glamour and apparent prosperity of the growing industrial cities. Not only was the city attracting their sons and daughters; it was exploiting those who remained on the soil. There, in town, lived the middlemen and speculators who took a parasitical cut of everything the farmer produced. There lived the absentee landlords growing rich on the labor of others. There were made laws that victimized the farmer: tariffs that protected industry and made the farmer pay more for what he bought, but that failed to underwrite the price of his crops; fiscal policies that shrunk the currency and made it even harder for him to pay his debts; tax laws that caused him to support his government disproportionately. Industrial monopolies were allowed to flourish, forcing upward the price of kerosene for his lamps,

Mottoes displayed at this Illinois Grange meeting compared the wages of a farmer ($.75 a week) to those of a Congressman ($7,000 a year) and urged "Brothers, let us organize & educate for knowledge is power." (Engraving after sketch by Joseph B. Beale in *Frank Leslie's Illustrated Newspaper,* August 30, 1873)

while homesteaders were limited to 160 acres of even the most wretched land. Stung by the many jokes and jibes at the expense of the "rube" or "hayseed," the farmer nodded his head in bitter agreement. He was indeed the victim.

The first sign of action on behalf of the farmer came in a manner that was highly typical of this period: the formation of voluntary organizations. The most widespread of these associations was the Patrons of Husbandry, founded in 1867 by Oliver H. Kelley, and known familiarly as the Grange. Originally attractive to the farmer as an antidote to his characteristic loneliness, the Grange featured elaborate ritualistic initiations, reminiscent of the Masons, and sponsored dances and picnics which became the highlights of rural social season. In addition to enjoying themselves with their neighbors, the farmers talked shop; it was not long before the Grange and its kindred organizations were sponsoring regular programs devoted to rural problems and, in some localities, acquiring libraries. By 1874 the Grange had 1,500,000 members, who were not only dancing reels and singing hymns together, but were exchanging ideas about home canning, crop rotation, and care of livestock.

The Grange's character as a social and occupational organization has remained to this day; what gave it a peculiar magnetism in the Age of Enterprise was its willingness to conduct economic experiments and to seek political action. The precise nature of this activity differed notably from region to region; but Grangers did organize cooperative stores to fight the merchandising middleman, build cooperative grain elevators to combat the monopolistic storage charges of the railroads, and experiment with dairy and ranch cooperatives of various kinds. Through the courts they pressed the "Granger Cases," which ended by establishing the government's right and responsibility to regulate the railroads. When the Grange lost some of its political momentum, the

Campaigners for William Jennings Bryan in 1896 and 1900 used the plow to represent their sympathy with the farm against Eastern bankers who wanted gold-based currency and industrialists whose monopolies were represented by the octopus. (Lithograph by Strobridge, 1900)

Farmers' Alliance and the Agricultural Wheel picked up the slack by organizing the farm vote, backing the Populist Party, and forcing agrarian issues into state and national legislatures. The impulse for a political party of, by, and for the farmers failed; but by the time the Populists joined the Democrats in supporting William Jennings Bryan in 1896, the farmer could be assured that his own interests would be represented in the nation's forums.

While farmers were showing their power at the ballot box, their government was responding to some of the rural needs. The Homestead Act itself had been a great boom, and in 1873 and 1877 it was amended in order to favor genuine settlers over speculators and to make possible the acquisition of larger spreads in areas where small farms were impractical. Beginning in the 1880s, farmers' institutes, modeled on teachers' institutes, were established in many states and offered the agricultural population technical training. The Hatch Act of 1887 allotted funds for the establishment of local experimental stations, and the Morrill Act of 1890 financed instruction in agriculture and mechanics. In 1889 the U.S. Commissioner of Agriculture was made a Cabinet member, and by 1895 ten states had their own departments of agriculture.

As General Robert E. Lee dramatized when he put down his sword to become a college president, education was the best friend a depressed rural region could have. Congress had already abundantly recognized this fact in the Morrill Land-Grant College Act of 1862, which endowed agricultural colleges with 30,000 acres of land for each Congressman and Senator in each state. Colleges founded under the provisions of this act were soon making notable contributions. One of the first to distinguish itself was Iowa State College of Agricultural and Mechanical Arts where the famous Henry Wallace family became adept at solving plant and soil problems. Here also was trained George Washington Carver, son of slave parents, who eventually went to Hampton

Institute in Virginia and began courses in farm management which had a great and constructive impact on Southern agriculture. Almost from their inception these "cow colleges," some of which have since grown into our greatest universities, changed the life of the farmer by giving his children inexpensive vocational training and by providing the brains behind the experimental stations and farmers' institutes.

Isolation was most effectively attacked by the combination of improved technology and government benevolence that produced the expanded mail system. Once the postal department resigned itself to annual deficits, as it did in the mid-1880s, the rural public was enabled to subscribe to magazines, newspapers, and bulletins without prohibitive added charges. The railroad mail car and the building of postal roads allowed the government to contemplate mail delivery to individual farms instead of the nearest town post office where the farmer had formerly been obliged to appear and sort through the contents of the mailbag himself. By the mid-1890s the government was experimenting with rural free delivery, and by 1900 nearly 2,000,000 people were being served on rural routes.

The growing convenience of the mails did more than keep the farmer better educated, informed, and entertained; it also changed his buying habits. With a fortunate sense of timing, Aaron Montgomery Ward entered the mail-order business in 1872. With a shrewd sense of advertising, he catered to the farmer's prejudice against credit and middlemen. Ward announced that he paid no store rent, hired no agents, and did business on a strictly cash basis. Endorsed by the National Grange, Montgomery Ward & Company boasted that its thriving business had saved the remote consumer millions of dollars. Soon Richard W. Sears, a farm boy turned railroad clerk, started a rival firm. Even more outspoken than Ward in his attacks on the farmer's enemies, he also captured the knack of describing merchandise in terms that appealed to the rural consumer. The 500-page Sears, Roebuck catalog introduced farmers to products they had never heard of, and sold everything from diapers to coffins to anyone who would tear the ad from the catalog and mail it in: satisfaction guaranteed.

Life on the farm was transformed in some cases by the lessons of scientific farming passed on through institutes, colleges, and associations. Almost every farm, however, was changed in some way by the impact of technology: better irrigation equipment, wire fencing, improved windmills. The humblest, yet the most important, invention of this decade was James Oliver's chilled iron plowshare, which cut through the ground so much more smoothly than its rougher predecessor that difficult terrain could be turned over with less effort than was previously required for routine tilling. The disc plow, the disc harrow, the riding plow, and the spring-toothed harrow were all refinements of earlier equipment which made them more efficient and more adaptable to local needs and conditions. Planters and seed drills replaced the picturesque sowing motion by which farmers had planted for ages; instead drawn vehicles opened a furrow, drilled a hole, planted and fertilized in one operation. The straddle-row cultivator enabled the farmer to double the amount of acreage he could keep under cultivation, and a series of patented improvements in the milling process made Minnesota the flour king of the world.

Visually the most spectacular change was in the process of harvesting, gathering, and threshing grain. Harvesting equipment before the Civil War had merely cut the grain and left it to be gathered, bound, and threshed in separate operations. First a self-rake reaper appeared which gathered the grain in bundles. A number of imperfect attempts finally led to the twine binder of John F. Appleby, Jacob Behel, and Marquis L. Gorham. This machine bound the grain bundles, knotted the twine, and deposited the bound grain in stacks. The McCormick Company turned to the manufacture of this type of binder in 1882 and sold over 15,000 machines the first year,

Stretching across the horizon, lines of harvesters which could cut, bind, and stack in a single operation changed farming into large-scale enterprise. (Halftone after a drawing by W. A. Rogers in *Harper's Weekly,* August 29, 1891)

demonstrating the importance of this machine in the expansion of the wheat belt into the West and Northwest. Threshing was also mechanized through the improvement and coordination of cutting, weighing, feeding, and blowing apparatus. By 1900 it was possible to observe steam- or mule-powered combines, operating on the ideally level plains of the wheat belt, cut and thresh thirty acres of grain in a single day. This spectacle, which a farmer of the 1860s could only regard with open mouth, foreshadowed the unprecedented efficiency of the twentieth-century American grain growers.

For the few, for the alert, for those fortunately placed, the new day of efficient specialization was already at hand. For much of rural America, however, farming in 1900 remained very similar to farming in 1865. The momentum for change had been provided: by technological progress, by the spread of education, by the organization of associations, and by the paternal hand of government. The new century promised great things; the farmers of the Age of Enterprise lived more on promises than on fulfillment.

Engraving after drawing by A. B. Shults in *Harper's Weekly,* August 25, 1883.

4 The Changing Community

IN 1860 there were but sixteen American cities with populations over 50,000; in 1900 there were seventy-eight, and New York City had passed Paris. Speaking for the older, small-town America, William Allen White recalled how the village tyrant took comfort from the jeers of the children as they passed him on the street. They knew his name and their attention gave him a sense of filling a recognized place. At about the same time a Midwestern neighbor of White's reacted to the newer urban life as follows:

> Alone I walk in the peopled city,
> Where each seems happy with his own;
> O friends, I ask not for your pity—
> I walk alone.

American communities were changing in both size and nature.

In a small, rural-oriented village, people lived in an individualistic, preurban way. They depended on one another rather than on established institutions. When someone fell ill it was the neighbors who helped out at home. If death occurred, the family, in consultation with the minister, made all the arrangements themselves. Whether the town was just a crossroads or a county seat, with a bandstand and a Civil War monument in its village square, it boasted very few public buildings. Perhaps the schoolhouse would have been the only one. Many of the villages were not incorporated and had only the most shadowy legal existence. Their records were kept by the county clerk; law was enforced by the sheriff and administered by a circuit judge. The mayor and the school board were the only town officials; and these were unpaid, part-time, and mainly of ceremonial importance. A villager in such a community might have been aware of local government only at election time, and of the federal government only when it brought him his mail.

The most important institution in the town would have been the church. Here records of births, baptisms, marriages and deaths were kept before the community took over this function. The church building was often used for meetings to discuss public issues, in very much the way town meetings had taken place since New England colonial days. Church services formed the center of holiday celebrations—Christmas, Easter, and Thanksgiving—as well as of the Sabbath observances. Ministers performed as marriage counselors, psychiatrists, and public-welfare officers. Almost any problem could have been considered the church's, and a conscientious pastor would at least have brought it to the attention of his flock.

The second most important institution was the general store. The principal port of call for the farmer's Saturday visit, it also served the community in a number of other ways. It dispensed nearly everything: groceries, hardware, farm implements, boots, drugs, soap and sundries, sewing supplies, yard goods, hats, brushes, books, stationery, shaving supplies, earthenware and glassware, used crates, fresh produce, tobacco, and—if temperance were not a local problem—cider and whisky. Villagers, even more than farmers, depended on this store for the stuff of life; and, although arguments in favor of cash transactions were plentiful, the difference between health and malnutrition often depended upon the storekeeper's willingness to extend credit. The store was also a news bureau. Here local happenings were passed from mouth to mouth, sometimes assisted by the presence of a notice board. Mail, delivered to these fourth-class post offices, was dumped on a table in the back, opened and read by the recipients right in the store, and shared immediately with the ever-present audience. The store was also the stage on which performed the various "drummers," traveling representatives of wholesale dealers, who earned the storekeeper's order by entertaining him and his customers with the latest political scandals and predictions, embellished accounts of personal interchanges with big-city celebrities, more or less faithful reports of commodity prices in other towns, and whispered parodies of song favorites intended for male ears only.

In the golden era of the country store, between the end of the Civil War and the 1890s, this marketplace also functioned as a men's club for the villagers. Having scanned the bulletin board and checked his mail, the morning arrival would step to the part of the counter where tobacco was kept. "Five- or ten-cent plug this morning, Albert?" the clerk would query; and the slicer would descend on the loaf of fruity "eatin' tobaccuh," producing a good two hours' worth of ruminating pleasure. To accommodate this popular diversion, the storekeeper- was obliged to fill a large crate with sawdust for a spitting box, although the sportier chewers demanded a seat in line with the stove door, where they could show off their marksmanship by sizzling a stream at the blaze. The caustic sign of one tired storekeeper asked chewers not to use the stove or floor, but to spit only on each other. With a checkers game and a practical joke now and then, the local characters often managed to spend generous portions of their days talking horse trades, home remedies, and political sagacity. In larger towns rival groups would assemble at the barbershop or tavern; but in the smaller towns the store would have served not only as a rural parliament on Saturday, but as an informal village council all week long.

Aside from the church and general store there were few formal institutions or services provided by the small village at the close of the Civil War. There might be a small hotel or tavern, a bank, and a newspaper and printing office. There would surely be a livery stable, a blacksmith's shop, a harnessmaker's, and a boot and shoe store where footwear was made to order. If a lyceum lecture or a traveling stage show were booked, the site would be either the village square or picnic grounds in summer; in winter the church, the school, or a lodge hall would be used. As a link with the outside world there would be a train station, a commercial wharf, or at least a warehouse where freight could be delivered by horse- or ox-drawn wagons. Of all the goods and services now expected from a community, only these few institutions existed to provide them. Otherwise these citizens depended on themselves, their families, the voluntary activities of their neighbors, and an infrequent trip to the big city.

During this era there were many communities which left even more to the individual than the sort of village just described. Wherever railroads were being built across sparsely settled territory, wherever railheads attracted trail herds, whenever mineral discoveries promised sudden wealth, there sprang up boom towns. In these boisterous male settlements, the community existed only in the sale of necessary tools— saddles or picks—and the provision of food and drink. Gaming tables and dancing girls soon appeared, but even a traveling judge was rare and the local marshal or sheriff was often as quick on the trigger as the men he was hired to control. The extreme do-it-yourself community spirit which pervaded these towns can be noted in one episode usually attributed to the legendary Judge Roy Bean, "the law west of the Pecos." The following dialog between the judge and a complainant is supposed to have transpired in his combination courtroom and barroom:

"What is the prisoner charged with?" Roy Bean asked.
"Stealing horses."
"Whose horses?"
"Mine."
"You sure about it?"
"Caught him at it."
"Who nicked his ear?"
"I did when he didn't stop."
"Poor shot, Jack, but if you had got him he would not have been properly finished as becoming as horse thief. It's my ruling that the prisoner is guilty. The rest is your business, Jack. You'd better buy him a drink before you string him up. Court is adjourned."

Self-reliance was the keynote in frontier justice just as surely as it was in prospecting.

The spirit of the boom town lived on for a while after the turn of the century in Alaska, but the kind of raw, isolated life that had dotted the advance line of the frontier was rapidly becoming outmoded by improved transportation and communication as well as by the population inundation. While they flourished, these towns made legends of countless Wyatt Earps and "Wild Bill" Hickoks, preserving a strain of individualism which ran against the grain of communal change.

The direction of change was toward a community which impersonally provided and regulated a great many more commodities and activities. Ever-growing cities, densely settled by newly arrived immigrants, needed supervision and arbitration. More important was the flood of new goods and services developed by invention and industry. By 1900, most large communities were providing electrical power and light, piped gas and deliveries of coal, telegraph and telephone service. Drinking water, at first sold from carts, was by the turn of the century being piped into most nonfarm homes. Surfaced roads, suitable for bicycles and automobiles, were still rare in rural areas but were becoming commonplace in cities. Bridges and tunnels brought rails everywhere, and improved terminals for boats and horse-drawn trucks added to the important buildings serving the public. Horse-drawn omnibuses and streetcars, cable cars, trolleys, elevated railways, and even one subway had appeared in answer to the problem of internal transportation. Sanitation and sewerage continued as largely unsolved problems, but at least some strides had been made. Scavenger pigs, which used to roam the streets freely, had been replaced by street-cleaning gangs, and some of the most abominable examples of filth and congestion had been removed.

One of the great problems of nineteenth-century communities was fire. Most American cities had grown of closely built structures which offered little resistance to flames. In pre-Civil War days fire sentries on watchtowers filled the night air with alarms which set off the mad competitive dash of proud and belligerent volunteer companies to the rescue. Although these firemen were highly skilled, they tended to vie rather than cooperate with one another. Thus, the blaze frequently roared to an unquenchable peak while the brave fireboys fought to see whose hose would get attached to the hydrant. Crowds grew to regard the fights between the companies as an attraction superior even to the sky-licking flames; and the giant Mose, powerful hydrant man of the Bowery Company, became a Bunyonesque hero so renowned that a highly popular series of plays was written about him. Such colorful antics, however, were not equal to the problems of late nineteenth-century cities, hardly one of which escaped a major fire. Pittsburgh, San Francisco, Boston, and Chicago were hosts to but a few of the major blazes. In the period from 1875 to 1900, each year saw the consumption by flames of $3 to $4 for every $1,000 of "burnable wealth." The twentieth-century figure would be less than half that.

The answer to this problem was sought in two directions: new technology and professionalization. Cincinnati, in 1853, became the first city to establish a salaried fire department, supported by the city and equipped with modern, steam-powered equipment. Other cities followed suit, and by 1900 volunteer departments remained only in suburbs and in smaller towns. Speedier methods of harnessing the fire horses were devised, signal boxes were installed, and chemical engines were introduced. The invention of the automatic fire-sprinkler system in 1877 got closer to the problem of stopping fires before they became uncontrollable; but the real answer came gradually, as wooden structures were replaced by those made of stone, brick, concrete, metal, and tile.

Growing cities also gave dimensions to the problem of law enforcement which placed it far beyond the competence of the sleepy night watchman or the part-time sheriff. Improved transportation had made the criminal mobile. According to an "itinerant policeman" of this period, crooks moved easily between well-established outlaw communities in Boston, New York, Philadelphia, Pittsburgh, Buffalo, Cincinnati, Cleveland, Detroit, Chicago, St. Louis and San Francisco. In predictable hordes they descended on fair and exposition cities prepared to pick pockets, pass counterfeit money, and otherwise victimize strangers in town. Criminal ranks were swelled by the children of immigrants who rubbed elbows with lawlessness in overcrowded slums, and whose ignorance of American customs and language made it more difficult for them to gain a livelihood inside the law. "Robbers' Roost" and "Murderers' Alley," described and photographed by Jacob Riis, were representative of slum areas in all major cities where police entered at their own risk.

In answer to these problems, full-time, uniformed, salaried police departments had been established by New York, Philadelphia, and Boston in the 1850s, and by other cities in ensuing years. Police departments, however, did not necessarily mean strict law enforcement, as many communities discovered. In New York the Reverend Charles H. Parkhurst made himself a national figure by consorting incognito with criminals and their police allies, then delivering his firsthand evidence of graft and connivance from the pulpit of the Madison Square Presbyterian Church. The underworld fought back by producing apparent evidence of Parkhurst's own compromised morals, thus giving journalists throughout the country some of the most lurid headlines of the century. Parkhurst's findings, however, were vindicated by the 1894 investigations of the Lexow Committee, and dramatized by the appointment of Theodore Roosevelt as police commissioner of New York City in 1895. Police problems resisted solution partly because of the generally inefficient character of urban government, and partly because the criminal community was better organized than its law-enforcing counterpart. Eventually police departments began to cooperate nationally. The earlier idea of a rogues' gallery of criminal photographs was enlarged and expanded. To this was added the Parisian method of identifying criminals through precise physical measurements. Better locks, vaults, and alarms made life more difficult for the lawbreaker and gave police better tools with which to fight the constantly mounting crime statistics.

A more successful extension of community responsibility was into the field of public education. Momentum that had gathered in the 1830s and '40s was recaptured with some impressive results. One after another, states passed compulsory education laws requiring, typically, children from the ages of eight to fourteen to attend school twelve to sixteen

weeks a year. Expenditures for public primary and secondary education rose from $63,000,000 in 1870 to $215,000,-
000 in 1900, allowing for an advance in the enrollment of
school-age children from 57 percent to 72 percent. While the
school term lengthened from an average of 132 to 144 days,
illiteracy dropped from nearly twenty to less than eleven percent.

What was life like for the schoolchild of the Age of Enterprise? In a rural environment, and especially in the South
where sparse population and poverty combined to keep
things relatively backward, school days were likely to be short
and hectic. Underpaid, poorly trained teachers in ungraded
schools did well to impart even the rudiments of learning. In
the cities of the North and West, however, the situation was
measurably brighter. Taxation for the purpose of education
was a more widely accepted principle, and the wealth of the
cities made schools much more impressive physically. The
three Rs were supplemented by courses in manual training,
domestic science, and physical education. The patriotic impulse that characterized reunion after the Civil War was
coupled with the idea of citizenship training, so that school
days often opened with the Pledge of Allegiance to the flag
and included classwork in American history and current
events. As the period progressed, more and more teachers
were trained to be more than disciplinarians instilling fixed
knowledge by rote. Many states even passed laws forbidding
corporal punishment in the classroom, presaging a day when
the hickory stick would evoke nostalgia rather than fear. Instead of motivating pupils by intimidation, the teacher was
charged with creating interest in the curriculum; and his task
was made reasonable by the addition of courses that would
demonstrably prepare the student for an adult life of working
and voting. With the national average of time allotted to
public education no better than five years in 1900, there
remained much to be done; yet, according to some impressive commentators, it was the system evolved during this era

Well-equipped machine shops were a part of the movement to ex-
pand the role of the school beyond the fundamental subjects and
make them into a broader training mechanism for citizenship and
craftsmanship. (Photograph by Frances B. Johnston, 189?)

that narrowed the gap between the educated and uneducated and made Americans in general the best-informed people in the world.

Although college in 1900 was still for the few, certain developments in higher education during these years showed that community responsibility for education was not to stop with high school. The 500-odd colleges that existed at the close of the Civil War had grown to nearly 1,000 by 1900, and the enrollment in these institutions had leaped from 50,000 to 350,000. More significant than this phenomenal growth itself was the shift in leadership from private to public institutions and the consequent democratization of higher learning. Small private colleges founded at midcentury, many of them denominational, were having troubles with financial and popular support—so much so that even during this period of booming education the number of colleges actually decreased between 1890 and 1910. Unless these colleges were buttressed by some act of great financial faith—as happened when John D. Rockefeller's bequest gave a new birth to the University of Chicago—they tended to grow only slowly if at all. State universities, particularly in the Midwest and in California, earned generous support from their legislatures and gathered enough academic momentum to rival the much older private institutions in the East. Furthermore, they opened college life to the many by adopting coeducation, by charging only token tuition, and by admitting high-school graduates without examination.

Before the Civil War colleges had offered rigid and rather unworldly curricula centered on mathematics and the classics. After the war, however, the colleges began to bring their environment into the classroom through instruction in modern languages, laboratory sciences, and social sciences. The increasing number of these new courses—together with the swelling need for them—had two important consequences. In the first place it settled the raging argument between the fixed course of study and the elective system in favor of the latter;

consequently, by the 1890s at least, most college students were able to choose their own courses during their final two years. In the second place, the new courses led to specialization on the part of the faculty, to increased scholarly productivity, and to the development of graduate programs. Johns Hopkins, Clark, and Chicago Universities led the way by importing German practices and developing them into the modern concept of graduate education. These programs enjoyed the participation of only a tiny fraction of the American population, but what went on in them affected the multitudes. It was here that the idea of evolution, subject to so much popular debate throughout these years, was accepted and applied beyond Darwin's limits. Science faculties came to a better understanding of nature and applied this knowledge to better methods for agriculture and industry and to an improved concept of germs, disease, and sanitation that was to prolong many lives, including that of President Cleveland. Although universities generally suffered when they became involved in politics, it was also true that social-science faculties at such universities as Chicago and Wisconsin were developing the answers to political and economic problems which candidates and voters would gratefully accept in just a very few years.

College life also contributed two new folk heroes to popular culture: the "college man" and the "coed." They contrasted strangely with the Joe Magaracs, Buffalo Bills, and John Henrys; in fact, they moved in an aura significantly different from that surrounding college students both earlier and later. Before the Civil War, the college man was depicted either as a faintly ministerial bookworm, or as a drunken vandal wasting his patrimony. By the 1920s he had become "Joe College," familiar, flippant, and harmlessly fun-loving. In between, he enjoyed a measure of respect and envy that proved to be unique. He was characterized as virile and erect, cleanshaven in a bearded age, clad in his private status symbol: the ribbed, turtlenecked sweater associated with the gridiron. His left hand suavely half-concealed the outlines of a huge curve-stemmed bulldog pipe. In his expression a friendly, slightly condescending candor overlay the twinkle of hidden knowledge, further symbolized by the glitter of the fraternity badge upon his manly chest.

His image reflected some facts of college life. Campuses and sports had fallen into each other's arms as though made for each other. Older sports grew in popularity: boxing, fencing, wrestling, rowing; new sports, especially football, owed their emerging national eminence almost exclusively to the colleges. Some of these sports continued to have snob appeal; but when 50,000 spectators gathered to watch the Princeton-Yale football game in 1893, it was obvious to everyone that the colleges had hit on something enormously popular. Some saw a danger in overemphasis on sports. It should be remembered, however, that the debating matches were just as central to college interests as the football matches, and that the first Williams College baseball weekend was accompanied by a chess tournament. Nor were Greek letters used accidentally to identify the branches of the spreading tree of college fra-

As early as 1876 cartoonist Thomas Worth was concerned lest college students spend their time seeking laurel wreaths for their brows at the expense of learning for the interior of their skulls. (Lithograph by Currier & Ives)

ternities that blossomed so fully during these years. To the undergraduate these clubs meant parties rather than studies; but he surely did not want Sigma Alpha Epsilon confused with the International Order of Odd Fellows, even though both may have prospered from that same American impulse to join. College and fraternity life both stood for initiation into the mysteries—academic as well as social; the age valued the mysteries. The head of a department store would be proud of what he had achieved with only a grade-school education; but as he approached retirement he would confidently put his affairs in the hands of a college man, expecting even greater things from his educated successor.

The coed was something brand-new. At the end of the Civil War the entire country was producing only 1,000 women college graduates annually. By 1900, four out of five colleges admitted women, and all varieties of degree-granting programs were open to them. In 1900 men received over four times as many degrees as women, which explains, among other things, why the coed attracted so much attention. She was depicted as a vigorous young lady and was often shown becomingly garbed for golf or tennis. Her every expression and attitude stamped her as the antithesis of her retiring, helpless Victorian sisters. She knew that a flying wedge was not to be shot at but tackled; she knew that a mashie was as appropriate on a golf course as a masher was in the stag line; she could enter a discussion of the backhand stroke without feeling that someone was being deceived. Nor was she upset by phrases such as "process of natural selection," "dynamic sociology," or "diphtheria bacillus." Informedly she mingled with the young men who were to lead the country into the twentieth century; furthermore, she mingled at the favorable —as her mother might hope—ratio of four to one. No wonder women's magazines became preoccupied with college life and stories. No wonder their pages were filled with detailed and avidly read instructions for young ladies who wished to cross the magic threshold into coeducationland.

The growing sense of community responsibility for education by no means ended with public schools and colleges.
The Chautauquas that served rural communities were joined
by the old Lyceum movement, revitalized under the leadership of James Redpath, in making lectures and extension
courses available almost everywhere. Throughout this era
they filled lecture platforms with muckraking journalists like
Lincoln Steffens, eminent foreign visitors like James Bryce,
social reformers like Jane Addams, and political spellbinders
like Robert M. La Follette and Theodore Roosevelt. In the
1890s summer sessions at leading universities began to compete with the Chautauqua camps; and special programs, like
those of Thomas Davidson on the Lower East Side of New
York City, brought learning to the urban underprivileged.
Prominent in giving city dwellers the opportunity to help
themselves through education were the Young Men's Hebrew Association, the Young Men's Christian Association
and their female counterparts.

Hand in hand with educational programs went the growth
of libraries until, in 1900, America boasted 1,700 collections
exceeding 5,000 volumes. Achieving public support even in
depression periods, the library justified itself on the grounds
that its readers would be instructed, inspired, and thus made
employable. No single force in this movement compared to
the generosity of Andrew Carnegie who, in 1881, began a
series of donations which eventually built 2,500 library
buildings throughout the country. The same impulse that
established libraries also opened the doors of art galleries,
founded conservatories of art and music, built elaborate concert halls and theaters. Prompted by pioneer planners like
Frederick Law Olmsted, cities began to provide public parks
with recreation areas, waterfront swimming and boating
facilities, zoological and botanical gardens.

In 1900 the government was still a generation removed
from taking a major responsibility in public health and welfare; but, continuing a crusade begun in the 1820s, private

agencies, universities, and churches expanded the facilities open to the ill and handicapped. Associated with the improvement of medical schools came an improvement in the number and nature of hospitals and clinics, such as those made famous by the realistic paintings of Thomas Eakins. The so-called "institutional church," dedicated to solving the social as well as the religious problems of its underprivileged parishioners, led in establishing settlement houses which fed the hungry, sought jobs for the unemployed, and cared for the aged. Special homes for orphans or old people grew out of some of these missions. The number of facilities available for the deaf and dumb, for the blind, and for the victims of incurable diseases grew throughout these years. One of the last groups to receive aid, the mentally ill, were being admitted in 1900 at the rate of 41,000 a year to state hospitals alone.

As the industrial revolution penetrated ever deeper into the manufacture of goods for the home and family, a parallel commercial revolution brought new areas of service to the

One of the early institutions to recognize the needs of a changing community was the New York Foundling Asylum, established in 1869 on 12th Street in lower Manhattan but moved, by the time of this Jacob Riis photograph in the late '80s, to a large building on uptown Lexington Avenue. (Riis Collection, Museum of the City of New York)

Characteristic of the "new city" were the modish and elaborate department stores, as depicted in this scene from opening day at Lord & Taylor's, a rather sad day for the American bill-payer. (Engraving after a drawing by Hyde, *Frank Leslie's Illustrated Newspaper*, January 11, 1873)

community. No longer did the housewife need to make her own clothes from yard goods bought at the general store or have herself fitted by a seamstress. She could rely instead on the mail-order catalog, or, if she lived in a good-sized community, on one of the sumptuous department stores—such as Wanamaker's in Philadelphia or Lord & Taylor's in New York—which were making shopping a new experience. In these modish emporiums, carpeted and upholstered elevators lifted the shopper gently and comfortably from floor to floor on which the latest coats, dresses, and underclothes were available in a multitude of styles. As the department store flourished, it added more and more items, until a family could not only dress itself but could furnish an entire home without leaving the confines of a single store. For merchandising the startling abundance of inexpensive manufactured items—from combs to toys, from corkscrews to picture frames—an empire of variety stores was beginning to gain a national foothold. The shelves of these five-and-ten-cent stores contained more objects than could ever have found their way into the crowded general and hardware stores.

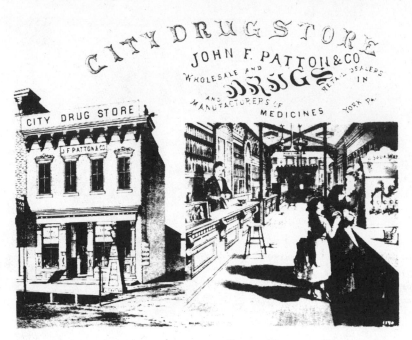

This pictorial advertisement for a small city drugstore done in about 1880 shows the first intrusions of brand-name advertising (the large "Pond's Extract" sign at the rear of the store) and of the soda fountain. Note the elaborate woodwork in the counters and shelf cornices. (Lithograph after a drawing by Ray)

Specialization also attacked the marketing simplicity of an earlier day. Where once the baking and butchering had been done at home or on a nearby farm, there now appeared bakeries and meat stores. Shops devoted only to selling candy or carriages, farm equipment or jewelry, replaced markets which had formerly carried a wide variety of wares. The concept of the general store was saved only by the appearance of the chain store, itself made possible by innovations in canning, packing, refrigeration, and transportation. Although the chain grocery stores and drugstores had but a bare beginning in this era, and although they carried what today would be considered a very limited inventory, they did allow for the introduction of standard packaging, brand-name advertising, national distribution, and high-volume, low-cost sales to the consumer. Eventually their stock of wares came to resemble nothing so much as an air-conditioned, sanitized, prepackaged version of the old country store. The local checkers-playing philosophers, of course, had been swept out with the pot-bellied stove; only the drugstore cowboys remained.

The full measure of change could be savored only in mushrooming cities which, in their newness and special characteristics, were unique to the Age of Enterprise. Before the days of large-scale manufacturing and centralized commerce, there had been no need for cities of such density. Nor would they have been possible without the technology that produced the skyscraper, the elevator, and the rapid transit. Suddenly, connected by rail, telegraph, and telephone lines, they responded as if by magic to the needs of an industrial age:

> An alder swamp, in thirty days, would grow into a public lawn. . . .
> An' fox trails into public streets, an' cow paths into boulevards!

City dwellers were fond of detailed maps which emphasized growth and vitality. Here Philadelphia, pushing beyond the Schuylkill River, had attention called to its smoking industrial chimneys. (Lithograph by Currier & Ives, 1875)

There was Chicago, fastest-growing of all the great new cities, which put itself proudly on display with its World's Columbian Exposition of 1893, revealing to thousands of startled visitors how a prairie by the lake had become a metropolis of 1,500,000 souls, brawling and broad-shouldered, outgrowing itself at every seam, as Carl Sandburg described it shortly after the turn of the century. There was Pittsburgh, which rose from tenth to seventh American city between 1870 and 1900, and which elicited spectacular descriptions from visitors arriving under its smoky umbrella and seeing in the fiery steel furnaces on its hillsides the searing flames of hell. New Orleans, with its Creoles, Cajuns, and ocean-going traffic, struck visitors as a new kind of cosmopolitan center with a rather Old Worldly aura of decadence. San Francisco, a meeting place for East and West, for frontier and civilization, began to take on its strangely Mediterranean character and to think of itself as an Athens by the Pacific. Cincinnati, losing its hog-butchering preeminence to Chicago, retained the seven-hilled charm of its river valley and began to take pride in the quality of song that arose from its German beer gardens on Sunday evenings. Cities whose importance depended solely on water transportation began to slide down the scale of relative wealth and population; but in their place came an entirely new crop: Detroit, 80,000 in 1870 and 286,000 in 1900; Minneapolis, 13,000 in 1870 and over 200,000 in 1900; and Los Angeles, which grew from 6,000 to 100,000 during those same years.

What was special about these Age of Enterprise cities aside from their new technology, their rapid growth, and their marks of individual coloring? To judge both from personal reactions and from historical statistics, the answer to this question lay in the extremes of wealth and poverty they harbored:

In a great, Christian city, died friendless, of hunger!
Starved to death, where there's many a bright banquet hall!

In a city of hospitals, died in a prison!
Homeless died in a land that boasts free homes for all!
In a city of millionaires, died without money!

Throughout most of his era it was the millionaires who attracted a lion's share of the attention. They wanted it that way.

As the great new fortunes of the industrial age began to accumulate, and as the older fortunes were passed on to heirs who were more interested in spending money than accumulating it, there developed a national rash of extravagant behavior which the economist Thorstein Veblen permanently labeled "conspicuous consumption." It seemed not enough for many of the wealthy just to have money; they set about to use it in the most conspicuous of ways. The way they housed themselves was typical, for they spared no expense to emulate the grandest models of European opulence. Troops of craftsmen from Italy arrived in Newport, Rhode Island, to carve marble and wood, paint murals on walls, and chase

Perhaps the most architecturally successful of the grand country homes of this period was William K. Vanderbilt's Biltmore, designed by Richard M. Hunt and completed in the early 1890s. Frederick L. Olmsted, planner of Central Park, did the gardens. (Photograph by Detroit Publishing Co., 1902)

Another critical success of the period can be seen in the third house from the left: the same Richard M. Hunt's design for the same Vanderbilt, this time to meet the requirements of a Fifth Avenue town house. The house was completed in 1881; the photograph (Detroit Publishing Company) was taken about 1890.

precious metals into modern fittings until seaside palaces like "The Breakers" stood as an unsurpassed monument to purposeless expenditures. The hills of San Francisco, the North Shore of Lake Michigan near Chicago, and the "Main Line" outside Philadelphia were all generously sprinkled with only slightly less extravagant examples of architectural largesse. William K. Vanderbilt not only reproduced in Asheville, North Carolina, a sumptuous version of a Loire Valley château, but earlier he had employed Richard Morris Hunt to adapt the same strain of French Gothic to the problem of a New York townhouse. Under the leadership of Hunt and the firm of McKim, Mead & White, millionaires made Fifth Avenue the most spectacular residential showplace in the land, with granite and brownstone palaces stretching northward with ever-increasing pretensions.

Life in these homes changed at mid-century from a private to a public affair, due primarily to the influence of James Gordon Bennett and his New York *Herald*. Setting out to mock the social life of the wealthy, he regaled his readers with lurid tales of what went on behind the potted palms at the fancy masked balls. Horrified socialites found that the only way to keep themselves from public dissection was to advertise expensively in the *Herald*, or else to connive with its owner to provide gossip concerning other bluebloods. As the years went on, Bennett tamed his stories, hired a society reporter who mastered a few French phrases and used them to flatter the subjects of his articles. By the time the Civil War had ended, society had become accustomed to seeing itself in print and seemed to feel rather good about it.

Bennett's son, James Gordon, Jr., illustrated the transformation; he was accepted almost without hesitation into the sporting set that had been most outraged by his father's public attention. Furthermore, his ingenuity in maintaining his activity at a high level of conspicuousness won the envious admiration of his peers. After all, no one else had thought to install on his yacht a padded stall, cooled by electric fans, whence a pedigreed cow could provide fresh milk daily to the seagoing celebrants. No one else could so suavely kidnap an entire Amsterdam theatrical company and keep it performing on the yacht for days. Walking through restaurants, he kept things lively by snatching tablecloths out from under their burdens; at night he could sometimes be seen perched nakedly atop a madly speeding coach. In the end he was too conspicuous for his own good. Making his New Year's calls in celebration of 1877, he went to the punchbowl several times too often and behaved so badly to a young lady that her brother saw fit, two days later, to horsewhip him in the street in front of the fashionable Union Club. The resulting duel proved farcical; Bennett was too shaken to take aim and his opponent deliberately wasted his shot.

Although Bennett's exploits shamed him from the country, his newspaper set a pattern for the coverage of society's elaborate fetes that was soon followed by all major urban journals. Ward McCallister, who drew up the original list of the "Four Hundred" persons constituting the true New York society, described the pains taken to transform the ballrooms of Delmonico's and even the opera house into areas where hundreds could be wined, dined, and danced. Costume parties were popular for the special efforts that could be lavished on the regalia. Tons of flowers and miles of electric wires were used to produce subtle sylvan effects. At the banquet on the roof of Madison Square Garden the night in 1906 when Stanford White was shot, the centerpiece was a live swan lake. Somewhat less publicly, if no less expensively, the rich disported themselves in elegant clubs and hotels, passing through the streets in laquered boughams, landaus, and phaetons drawn by blooded and immaculately groomed horses.

The "Four Hundred" were not totally unassailable. The New York *World* described how Mrs. John R. Drexel combined her artistic instinct with Mr. Drexel's money in order to gain social prominence. Her principal tactic seems to have been regular opera attendance in a well-placed box, gowned and coiffured each evening in original and tasteful splendor. When Mrs. Drexel achieved the ultimate social acceptance it would be national news. In a place as remote from New York society as Mobile, Alabama, the newspaper devoted most of one 1889 issue to identifying the 282 marriageable ladies of the Social Register and tabulating their personal as well as financial assets. It was of some concern to this paper that only 200 marriageable males were available at a comparable social level. Of course, as rich American ladies discovered, there was always Europe with its annual crop of titled young men; and, when a match was made, the society pages tingled with the strangely undemocratic rhetoric which made an idyl of the process by which a "simple American girl" (whose father was worth only $4,500,000) could become an English duchess or an Italian countess in families where history was readily exchanged for solvency.

Americans brought back from Europe not only titles, but also paintings, sculpture, libraries, elegant clothes, manufactured family trees, and—in the case of Andrew Carnegie—a whole castle. Some of the rich led quiet, sober lives (J. P. Morgan's most public appearances were as a front-row hymn-singer at the Moody-and-Sankey revivals); many spent generous portions of their wealth for schools, charities, libraries, and museums from which the public benefited notably. Yet the record of this first age of industrial affluence shows it to have been a time when the rituals of polite society and the frivolous display of wealth were matters of broad and absorbing interest. Everyday life for the members of the elite in American cities seems to have been a constant round of art-collecting and palace-building, promenades in town and weekends at the watering places, costumes and cotillions, menus and decorations, entertaining and being entertained. Everyday life for other Americans, to an extent unequaled before or since, included gawking at the homes and yachts of the wealthy and reading endlessly about their activities in newspapers and magazines.

Turning from the society page, the newspaper reader in the 1890s might notice some attention being given to city dwellers at the other extreme from the Morgans, Drexels, and McAllisters. Jacob Riis, the police reporter who did the most to throw journalistic light on these people, called them "the other half." His terminology was statistically apt, at least in New York City, where over 1,500,000 people were living in some 43,000 tenements in lower Manhattan. Every city had its slums, but none teeming with so many varieties of victims as the environs of Baxter, Hester, and Mulberry streets. Slums were produced by a combination of immigrant pressures, corrupt city government, exploitative employers, greedy landlords, and unrealistic legislation poorly enforced. In all these commodities New York easily led the field.

Immigrants flocked to American shores throughout this period, particularly in the 1880s and 1890s, when they averaged close to 400,000 annually. Furthermore, as the century neared its end, the national origin of these immigrants began

With flash powder and prose Jacob Riis called journalistic attention to the New York slums. Riis often posed his supposed "candid" shots, but the misery he described was real. This 1888 photo was captioned "A Baxter Street Alley."

to shift pronouncedly from the "old" predominance of Germans, Irish, and other Northwest Europeans, to a "new" immigration of Russians, Poles, Italians, and other Southeastern Europeans. In the last forty years of the century annual immigration had quadrupled; during these same years migration from Great Britain decreased by half, while Southeastern Europeans were arriving at 100 times their former rate. This meant not only that large numbers of resourceless people were being crowded into the port cities of the East Coast, but that many of these people spoke little English and were ill equipped to establish themselves in a land that differed from their own in religious, economic, and political values. To the eye of the artist these foreign groups formed themselves into picturesque and exotic groupings. To the immigrant himself, however, the picture was one of helpless exploitation with only the unseen hope for the next generation prompting him to live on in his abysmal surroundings.

To the city politician these blocks of foreign-born poor

were often a godsend. In a day when the urban "bosses" were suffering the journalistic exposures of Lincoln Steffens and the cartoon vilifications of Thomas Nast, there was a need for entrenched power. The boss soon found that by establishing in slum districts a "ward heeler" who knew the language and habits of the neighborhood, he could count on a controlled vote in exchange for a few lumps of coal in winter, a kind word at a wake, a free barrel of beer at a wedding. Many services to which the slum dweller was freely entitled were presented to him as special privileges. In order to get his trash removed or his water turned on, he would have to wait on the boss's local representative and pledge political regularity. If, eventually, he opened a store or saloon, he found that only a record of faithful contributions to the party coffers would change the attitude of city officials from harassment to cooperation.

If the political system tended to entrap the slum dweller, so did the economic system. Wages in factories were unbelievably low, attuned to a labor force of women, children, and foreigners who did not know enough to bargain or change jobs. Stephen Crane, in his slum novel, *Maggie: A Girl of the Streets,* included an unforgettable description of Maggie's resentment against the foreman of the small shirt factory where she and her fellow seamstresses had been reduced to hapless pieces of machinery with only daydreams to keep themselves human. Even worse than the sweatshops were the conditions accepted by those who did piecework at home, filling their ill-ventilated rooms with lint and thread from the minute sewing and weaving operations they performed for only pennies a day. For the cigar maker in his basement and for the tie maker in her loft, the day ended not by the clock or the sun, but only with total fatigue. With such alternatives, many turned to the criminal's cunning, the beggar's idleness, or the scavenger's ingenuity. In the 1880s and 1890s the slums began to spawn strikes, marches, boycotts, and other signs of unrest. Thus, to the horrors of low wages

Another Riis photograph (about 1900) shows an immigrant family all making cigars in their overcrowded slum quarters. Unlike most tenement families, they had a room with outside windows.

and overwork was added the peril of violence at the hands of demonstrators, troops, and policemen.

According to most observers, however, it was the tenement housing itself which really defined and perpetuated the slum. Tenements began, in most cities, when formerly respectable neighborhoods were abandoned and their capacious residences turned into habitations for ten families instead of one. As different levels were shut off from each other, some occupants lost the use of water and plumbing. Rooms too were divided, and soon most tenants found themselves windowless. When landlords ran out of older houses, they made even worse tenements out of the former servants' quarters on the alleys; or they deliberately built flimsy tenements with an eye only to heavy occupancy and low maintenance. Building codes in existence would have prevented the

The Salvation Army offered hot soup and prayers to slum dwellers and appealed to the charitable sympathies of potential benefactors. (Reproduction of watercolor by G. A. Davis, *Frank Leslie's Illustrated Newspaper*, December 20, 1894)

worst of these abuses, but it was a rare city where they were enforced.

New Yorkers, alarmed by their slums before other urbanites, passed statutes as early as 1867. One, in 1879, required better light and ventilation and led to the so-called "old law" tenement built with a dumbbell-shaped floor plan in order to accommodate air shafts. This type of building, encouraged for the best of motives, soon became one of the worst of all slum dwellings. The air shafts, inaccessible from the ground, became vertical refuse pits, breeding germs and rodents. Soon the air-shaft windows had to be nailed shut. Eventually these air shafts served only to ventilate the fearsome fires that swept through blocks of these buildings with the suddenness of a bomb. When the New York housing commission met in 1900, after thirty-three years of legislated

tenement reform, it concluded that the situation was somewhat worse than before the first enactment.

Life in these blighted areas was as tawdry as one can imagine. Poverty and malnutrition were the universal conditions.
Disease followed inevitably and suffering was sometimes
compounded by prejudice.

> Well do I recollect [wrote Jacob Riis] the visit of a
> health inspector to one of these tenements on a July day
> when the thermometer outside was climbing high in the
> nineties; but inside, in that awful room, with half a dozen
> persons washing, cooking, and sorting rags, lay the dying
> baby alongside the stove, where the doctor's thermometer
> ran up to 115 degrees! Perishing for want of a breath
> of fresh air in this city of untold charities! Did not the
> manager of the Fresh Air Fund write to the pastor of an
> Italian Church only last year that "no one asked for Ital-
> ian children," and hence he could not send any to the
> country?

One section of lower New York was known as the lung
block, because of the exceptional number of tuberculosis victims; and, although slum statistics were as unreliable as the
subofficial lives of the slum dwellers made them, it is easy to
believe Riis' estimate that infant and child mortality rates
were twice the average. Shocked as he was by filth and
disease, Riis was even more appalled by the mental and
moral scars of a slum upbringing. Left to their own devices
from an early age, many slum children never even enrolled
in school; if they did it was only for a few months. The
enforced crowdedness of the streets and rooms brought them
into early contact with the lowest aberrations of human behavior. Observing the desperation, shiftlessness, and crimi-
nality of their elders, forced to scrounge and scrape for a
living almost from infancy, the children of the slums saw the
road of life as impassable as the east face of Mt. Everest.

Typical of this era was a tendency to sentimentalize urban poverty rather than to do something about it. The cover for this maudlin song, "The Little Wanderer," was made by adding lithographed patches and tatters to a drawing that was not sufficiently pitiable for Victorian taste. (Lithograph after a photograph after a drawing by F. Crow; J. H. Bufford, 1866)

Perhaps the true miracle of the slum experience was in the growth to self-respecting adulthood of even an infinitesimal fraction of its polyglot population.

Even for those who did not live in tenements, slums were a fact in everyday life. Americans throughout the nation felt the consequence of their existence: in the epidemics they bred, in the political empires they supported, in the labor market they undermined, and in the crime networks they quartered. For most of these years Americans accepted the slums in the spirit of the Biblical injunction that the poor ye shall always have with you. The tradition of self-help meant that the industrious would overcome their environment; the popular interpretation of Social Darwinism indicated that outsiders should not interfere, but should let the fit survive. Poverty was even sentimentalized. Match girls and newsboys were made the pathetic centers of songs and melodramas as they forced their ill-shod feet through the slush of winter streets in order to eke out a daily ration for an invalid mother. Pressing their worn and grimy faces against the steaming windows behind which sat the wealthy at sumptuous boards, these scrawny waifs brought ready tears to many a Victorian eye. Before this era had ended, however, a changing attitude was evident. No longer was it serenely hoped that private charities, model tenements, or church-sponsored settlements would cure the blight of slums. The muckraking camera and pen of Jacob Riis, the stories of Jack London, Stephen Crane, and many others made it clear to readers everywhere that the problem was too serious and widespread for individual, haphazard solution.

The simple, personal life of small-town America survived this era in boom towns, cow towns, and mining towns. One of the great changes in the everyday life for most Americans, however, was that wrought by changes in the community itself. Many thousands moved into the growing cities, many thousands more stayed to grow with them. By 1900 they found themselves living in a communal setting which contrasted sharply with what they had probably known in 1865. In place of a rather loose and causal community structure, they now turned toward the impersonal government or corporation to provide them with water and heat, sewerage and light, elevators and elevateds, machine-made clothes and factory-canned foods. It was a life of interdependence accentuated by technology, rather than a life of independence assured by distance. The new community freed the individual from some of the drudgery and danger of the past, but it made him dependent on the welfare of the community at large. Somewhat reluctantly, as the century closed, he saw the need for a new kind of responsible, collective civic conscience.

An apparently mild evening of variety acts like this one in Cheyenne might end in a legendary frontier-town brawl. The scarcity of females and the wearing of hats indoors showed that civilization had yet to come to this part of the West. (Engraving in *Frank Leslie's Illustrated Newspaper*, 1877)

Photograph by Frances B. Johnston, Detroit, 1903.

5 Leisure and Popular Taste

THE CHANGING community, against a background of
changing technology, produced an inevitable change in
patterns of leisure-time activity. Urbanization brought
people together in dense centers of population, and
improvements in local transportation made it possible for
them to assemble conveniently at a given place and time.
Improved printing, cheaper mails, telegraph and telephone
service put people in quick touch with what was going on.
The growing concept of advertising encouraged sponsors of
recreational activities to publicize their efforts, and capital
investments in public entertainment were stimulated by the
possibility of assembling large groups of paying customers in
the capacious stadiums and auditoriums made practical by
new building techniques. For exceptional events—expositions, annual conventions—the railroads now brought participants from all over the countryside, often at specially reduced fares.

139

Furthermore, the population was shaping itself into new modes of life which drastically affected the amount and nature of their free-time diversions. Labor-saving devices in the home and a shrinking work week gave new opportunities for planned recreations; Sunday, no longer a day of enforced inactivity, added importantly to each week's leisure time. Living in apartments, row houses, or relatively small city dwellings, urbanites were inclined to look outside the home for entertainment. Nor were they as apt to confine their social life to a neighborhood as they once had been. The movement of the population had destroyed many residential patterns; even if a family had not itself changed residence, it would almost inevitably have acquired a new set of neighbors. Family ties, for reasons discussed in Chapter Seven, weakened almost as much as neighborhood loyalties. Thus, to an increasing degree, city dwellers of the 1880s and '90s left home in the evening or on the weekend not as members of a family or residents of a particular block, but as individual, anonymous middle-class Americans looking for ways in which to lose their anonymity and fill the time which their parents had spent in productive labor.

When two Greeks meet they open a restaurant, the saying goes. When two Americans met, at least during this golden age of fraternalism, they founded an association. Some of these groups had, or came to have, a serious economic or political purpose, as did the Patrons of Husbandry. Like the farmers, workingmen saw their organizations change character during this period from the principally fraternal Knights of Labor to the American Federation of Labor, which had industrial bargaining as its chief purpose. Even an organization like the League of American Wheelmen, founded to bring together people who liked the same sport, developed into an important pressure group on behalf of paved roads. In the center of the associational picture, however, were organizations which existed just to get the boys (or girls) together and have a time.

These primarily social and usually secret societies existed only in small numbers prior to 1880, but between that year and the turn of the century close to 500 new orders were founded. Every fifth American adult male belonged to one of these clubs in the 1890s, according to a contemporary estimate; and this seems a safe guess when there were over 5,000,000 registered members in 70,000 local lodges, not counting the 900 college fraternity and sorority chapters, which claimed over 150,000 members. The largest was the International Order of Odd Fellows, imported from England in 1819, which had over 800,000 members by 1900. Next in numbers and probably first in annual budget were the Freemasons, who kept a distinct anti-Catholic tinge throughout these years of the New Immigration. Many Americans were concerned at the growing joiners' craze which was producing a mass of citizens who had taken secret pledges they might hold dearer than church and country. Examples were cited of lodgemen who had sacrificed careers and victimized families in order to promote the greater brotherhood.

Yet there was a good side as well. In the days before insurance and government relief agencies, these societies helped their members find employment, supported needy brethren, paid illness and death benefits to widows and orphans, and provided funeral and burial insurance. Furthermore, their charters seldom contained any articles antipathetic to the national goals and interests, and even when they did few members took them seriously. In fact the lodge experience offered many members their most direct training in representative government. In all, the fraternal movement produced two kinds of fools: those who became hypnotized by their own nonsense and wasted substantial portions of their adult lives at childish games, and those who alarmed themselves out of all proportion to the negligible threat embodied in this harmless search for brotherhood. The fools were the exceptions. For most members, a night at the lodge was an occasional lark and, probably, a very useful safety valve. When the size and complexity of the industrialized city seemed to threaten a man's self-recognition, he restored himself with the reassuring ritual of signets and swords, aprons and helmets, strange clasps from familiar hands.

Sometimes more serious of purpose, but often more pretentious in titles and ritual, were the war veteran and patriotic societies. The Grand Army of the Republic, founded in 1866, petitioned for veterans' pensions and aided needy war victims. The hereditary societies—Daughters of the American Revolution, Colonial Dames, Society of Mayflower Descendants—stressed ancestral virtues and genealogical ties.

The formation of the General Federation of Women's Clubs in 1889 gave evidence that female associations had by no means been limited to auxiliaries of male societies. The programs and purposes of these ladies' clubs differed widely. For some a club meeting meant an afternoon of progressive euchre, one of the many ancestors of contract bridge. For others it meant a trip to the settlement house in the slums where charitable work was done. What most of these groups had in common was an interest in self-culture. The "new woman" was conscious of her new opportunities and, in general, used her leisure to take advantage of them. Some clubs centered on the home, studying the latest practices in what was newly christened "domestic science," listening to decorators tell them how to achieve modish interiors, or following landscape gardeners on tours of their flowering triumphs in the hope of back-yard imitation. Other bands of ladies descended determinedly on museums and historic sites, catalogs and guidebooks in hand. Cultural values from remote places and times were brought to their lecture rooms by means of drawings and magic-lantern slides. Most of these clubs were not so much interested in bringing women to the ballot box as they were in bringing them out of the kitchen and into the living room where they could take full part in the elevated conversation of mixed groups. Their most important function was to make their members conscious of education as a continuing concept.

Education was the principal weapon employed by the most influential of all women's organizations of this era, the Women's Christian Temperance Union, founded in 1874. It was the conviction of Frances E. Willard that victory for the humane causes she espoused would come only with the next generation; hence this remarkable woman, who dominated W.C.T.U. policy from her election to national presidency in 1879 until her death in 1898, directed her main efforts toward getting control over the administration and curriculum of public schools. Frances Willard grew up a rough, ready, irreligious tomboy. She was converted to religious commitment by a vision she experienced during a serious illness and steered to a life of public service by the failure of her one serious romance and the death of her beloved sister. Her trust in the efficacy of education emerged naturally from her highly successful career as a teacher at Evanston College for Ladies and Northwestern University into which her college became absorbed. Although she failed as its president to keep her college alive, she proved a dynamic and efficient administrator of the W.C.T.U. At her death it had 10,000 branches and 500,000 members. Recognized around the world was the white ribbon its members wore as a pledge of purity against alcoholic drink. Miss Willard was hardly exaggerating when she replied to a hostess who offered her wine with dinner, "Madam, two hundred thousand women would lose somewhat of their faith in humanity if I should drink a drop of wine."

After the great temperance crusade before the Civil War swept through the North, there was an almost wholesale desertion of the cause. By 1868 only Maine had kept its antebellum law. Prohibition Party candidates ran every four years beginning in 1876, but they never got more than 2.24 percent of the popular vote, and not a single electoral vote. Yet, as in the suffrage movement, there was widespread

The crusade for temperance and prohibition gave focus to many feminine associations and kept alive the spirit of humanitarian reform during an era when there were few popular causes. (Lithograph by Currier & Ives, 1874)

progress on the local level. Using the weapon of local option in rural areas and of high license fees in the cities, the enemies of drink had succeeded in restoring five states (Maine, New Hampshire, Vermont, North Dakota, Kansas) at least temporarily to statewide prohibition and had achieved limited or local prohibition measures in more than half the rest. With the formation of the Anti-Saloon League in the 1890s, the nation was about to learn what a well-financed, well-organized associational lobby could accomplish in Washington against the resistance of the entrenched special interests which had so easily defeated national temperance movements over the years.

All this organized activity for and by women, coupled with the entry of women into business and professional life and the publicity given female activity in periodicals of all kinds, had made the age highly self-conscious about the status of half its population. A phrase, "the new woman," took on a complicated significance which was sneeringly cataloged in these lines published in 1898:

Then shout hurrah for the woman new,

With her rights and her votes and her bloomers, too!
Evolved through bikes and chewing gum,
She's come! . . .

Many men and women alike reacted to the emancipation
of women as though it were the masculinization of women—
ludicrous, degrading, and annoying. Cartoons and satiric
sketches picturing men and women in reversed roles gave
constant testimony to the edgy preoccupation which accompanied this movement. But considerable print was expended
on behalf of this new woman, too:

> She studies all the questions of the day,
> And gives these problems of her earnest thought;
> Wise plans for woman unto her are brought,
> Which shed new light on her advancing way.

Opposed in spirit to reform associations were the new
country clubs, which also found many members during the
Age of Enterprise, particularly in suburban and resort areas.
Here middle- and upper-class Americans indulged themselves

Along with temperance, the movement toward women's suffrage
occupied the center of the reform stage. Women were first granted
the vote on issues that related to education. (Engraving in *Frank
Leslie's Illustrated Newspaper*, December 20, 1879)

Men did not know whether to fear or admire the "new woman" as she began to emerge. The bitter humor of an imagined reversal of roles was a constant theme during this uneasy transition. (Lithograph by Currier & Ives, 1869)

in sports which required expensive equipment, such as polo, or extensive space, such as golf. Tennis, a recent import from England, suffered the stigma of being considered a soft game for women and frail men and therefore found its principal home in private clubs rather than in the public parks. Club-houses, originally small shacks for changing clothes, grew to include ballrooms and restaurants where elegant food and drink were served. Soon families were considering the country club the center of their social life, using its facilities to entertain friends and even to cater to formal wedding receptions.

The downtown equivalent of the country club was the men's club. Some men's clubs housed indoor athletic facilities; all featured a grand sitting room where the latest periodicals were made available and overstuffed chairs allowed for quiet conversations or fitful naps. As opposed to the lodges, which often rented their modest quarters, men's clubs indulged themselves in the most impressive architecture they could obtain. The expensive firm of McKim, Mead & White, famous for adapting Renaissance motifs to the sidewalks of

New York, designed no less than four imposing men's clubs:
The Century, for successful artists and writers; the Metropolitan, for millionaires of whom J. P. Morgan approved; the
Harvard, for alumni of that university living in New York;
and the University, which became one of a series of urban
clubs to which graduates of any college could be proposed
for membership. Here a man could take a business prospect
for lunch or an out-of-town visitor for dinner and confidently
expect him to be impressed by the decor, the service, and by
his host's first-name intimacy with the celebrities he might
pass in the halls. Here a man could sit around a table with
members who shared his background and happily reinforce
his own prejudices.

Those who were concerned at the way in which clubs were
outnumbering churches might have saved themselves despair
by observing what was happening to the churches themselves. Here too the organizational impulse was at work. Not
only were ministers organizing groups to support peace, temperance, interdenominationalism, and political socialism, but
they were sponsoring a variety of associational activities
among their congregations. This activity owned something to
an emerging religious philosophy known as the "social gos-

Golf was one of the newly popular games which allowed men and
women recreational companionship and which led, eventually, to
more sensible casual clothing for women. (Reproduction of watercolor by W. T. Smedley, *Harper's Weekly*, July 31, 1887)

Overfurnished, overstuffed, overdecorated rooms like these formed the social center of the fashionable end-of-the-century men's clubs. (Photograph by George C. Boldt, 1902)

pel," which held that the church should extend itself beyond matters of theology and strictly spiritual leadership into all areas that affected the social environment of their parishioners. Followers of this gospel projected their churches into labor education, slum rehabilitation and other social work, calling on groups within the church to organize support for these special projects. Instead of a Sunday school for the youth alone, adults were encouraged to meet before and after service to discuss current political and economic problems in a religious atmosphere. Children were no longer tested by exposure to hour-long sermons, but were arranged into age groups and induced to make the church a center for social as well as religious activity. Soon many churches boasted large rooms which could be used as gymnasiums and even theaters.

and ballrooms. Very much in tune with the social gospel were the Young Men's Christian Association, the Young Men's Hebrew Association and their female counterparts, with their mixture of self-culture, athletics, crafts, and social activities against a background of moral purpose.

Next to the urge to form clubs, the most distinctive leisure-time impulse was toward playing or watching sports. In addition to the two great crazes of the era, bicycling and croquet, participation in tennis and golf increased throughout the era and there was a renaissance of hunting, fishing, hiking, and boating. Interest in swimming, track and field events was on the rise. Archery and target shooting were but two of the minor sports which attracted legions of followers. Basketball, the only major sport of modern days that clearly originated in America, was invented in 1891 by Dr. James Naismith, an athletic instructor at the International Y.M.C.A. Training School of Springfield, Massachusetts. Within a few years it was being played in schools and Ys from coast to coast as a welcome indoor interlude between the outdoor sports of spring and fall. Roller skating, imported as a pastime for the social elite of New York City, was soon attracting crowds to

Cycling was not only a means of transportation and a gentle diversion but also a fiercely competitive sport. Here, as late as 1890, men raced the dangerous but speedy old high-wheelers at a fairground track. (Photograph by George Barker)

This tableau was photographed (by Frances B. Johnston) in a Washington, D.C., high school in the 1890s. The expectation of a low-scoring game seems indicated by the net completely fastened at the bottom.

gigantic rinks in Chicago, San Francisco, and other cities. Having sedately circled the hardwood floor, skaters paused to admire solo exhibitions like "Professor" A. E. Smith's astounding "Philadelphia Twist," a maneuver during which he gradually split his speeding legs until he could rest his head sideways on an almost horizontal calf.

The growth of sports had particular meaning for the female population. Many sports provided a socially acceptable opportunity for activities that could be enjoyed equally by both sexes. Victorian conventions kept flirtations rather tame by modern standards, but at least the golf course and tennis court showed more sides of a partner's personality than would have been visible on a formal Sunday visit. Furthermore, sports inevitably demonstrated the cumbersome restraints of fashionable female attire. Lifting several pounds of ornamented velour when serving a tennis ball or attempting to swim while anchored by yards of waterlogged cotton, women firmly decided not only that simpler street clothes were in order but also that concessions would have to be made to freedom and mobility even at some sacrifice in total modesty.

Aside from the growing number of popular sports, the distinctive thing about them was their expanding audience. Horse racing, long a magnet to viewers and gamblers, was revived by the investments of some well-to-do families in establishing thoroughbred lines. By the 1890s lengthy racing meets occupied most of the summer and were punctuated by prestige races such as the Kentucky Derby at Louisville's Churchill Downs, the Belmont Classic, and the elegant features at the Jerome Park Jockey Club. Boxing too had been an antebellum favorite, dominated by Negroes from the Southern plantations. After the war there was a period when the almost universal laws against boxing were enforced, and even the championship fights had to be staged clandestinely in out-of-the-way places. With the acceptance of the Marquess of Queensberry rules in the 1880s, prizefighting lost some of its stigma, and by the end of the century workingmen were taking their girls to boxing clubs where exhibitions

Lithograph by Currier & Ives after a drawing by J. Cameron of the unrivaled sports hero of the age, John L. Sullivan, the year after he won the world's heavyweight championship (1883).

were staged in a small ring that was used, in between bouts, for dancing and variety acts.

The immense popularity enjoyed by boxing in the 1890s was due, more than anything else, to the flamboyant personality of the Boston Strong Boy, John L. Sullivan. Winning the title from Paddy Ryan in 1882, he established himself as a pugilistic giant in his brutal seventy-five-round victory over the doughty Jake Kilrain. This last of the great bare-knuckle championship bouts earned the winner $20,000, a diamond-studded championship belt, and all the publicity he needed for a profitable national tour on which he offered $1,000 to anyone who could stay in the ring with him four rounds. While Sullivan was battling, boasting, and carousing—he staggered into the ring for one fight in full evening dress, including diamond shirt studs—the more restrained "Gentleman Jim" Corbett was quietly training at the San Francisco Olympic Club. Corbett was using the new five-ounce gloves, and perfecting the science of boxing that was to distinguish this sport from the brawling bare-knuckle days that had just ended. Sullivan, caught in a period of transition, was defeated by the wily, weaving and bobbing Corbett with his methodical jabs and counterpunches. Unprepared for the sudden dethronement of one of its greatest heroes, the nation mournfully chanted this parody of a currently popular Broadway song:

Photograph by S. R. Stoddard of a football game between Cornell and Rochester, October 19, 1889. Note the absence of shoulder pads, helmets, and the nearly upright stance.

John L. has been knocked out! the people all did cry.
Corbett is the champion! how the news did fly.
And future generations, with wonder and delight,
Will read in hist'ry's pages of the Sullivan-Corbett fight.

Soon, however, there was a new hero at the center of a new legend. For, on St. Patrick's Day of 1897, in a fight held over the protests of Frances Willard, Robert Prometheus Fitzsimmons knocked out Corbett with his devastatingly scientific "solar-plexus" punch.

Although football attracted considerable public attention during this period for its roughness and professionalism, it remained the property of the colleges. The impressive crowds which gathered at Ivy League games were, more often than not, described on the society rather than the sport pages. Prior to one Yale game a New York paper ran a feature unthinkably entitled "The Journal's Woman Reporter Trains with the Little Boys in Blue." The emergence in the 1890s of strong teams at service academies, at larger state universities, and at private universities in the South and Far West showed that football would soon become a national, middle-class sport; but the Age of Enterprise sports fan let nothing rival his love for baseball. He sang songs about it ("Slide, Kelly, Slide!"), made riddles about it ("What has eighteen feet and catches flies?"), and spent his sunny afternoons playing and watching it. By the end of the century there was hardly an American who could not cite the base-running exploits of that fabulous rookie, Honus Wagner, compare the managerial genius of "Cap" Anson and Ned Hanlon, or recite the full text of the ballad that ends:

Oh, somewhere in this favored land the sun is shining bright,
The band is playing somewhere, and somewhere hearts are
    light;
And somewhere men are laughing, and somewhere children
    shout,
But there is no joy in Mudville—mighty Casey has struck out.

This scene by the New York Lithograph Co. ornamented the 1887 schedule of the home team. It would be reasonably familiar to any frequenter of the recently demolished Polo Grounds except for the transition from stylish coaches to rowdy bleachers in left field.

In spite of the popular myth concerning Abner Doubleday and Cooperstown, New York, no one seems to know exactly where and how baseball descended from older games involving balls, sticks, and bases. A gradual evolution had produced something very close to the present game at least by the 1840s. Like roller skating, it was at first a fashionable exercise played in natty blue trousers and straw hats and followed with a formal dinner. It was not long, however, before Boston truckers were scheduling games on the Common at 5:00 A.M. so they could finish in time for work. The Civil War interrupted the development of local leagues but spread the game's popularity by bringing addicts and innocents together in Union and Confederate prisons and camps. A prewar tendency toward professionalism was made overt in 1869 when the Cincinnati Red Stockings toured the country as the first avowedly professional team. Captained by Henry Wright, a former paid cricket bowler, they defeated their opposition by lopsided scores, losing not one game all season. Other teams followed suit; in 1871 the players reorganized on a professional basis, and in 1876 the first effective league was made up of teams from New York, Philadelphia, Hartford, Boston, Chicago, Louisville, Cincinnati, and St. Louis. For a while the organizational history of baseball was complicated by interference from gamblers and by attempts of players to take over the game from the club owners. But the National League persisted and, after the American Association collapsed in the '90s, the National League was joined by the Western League in 1899—renamed the American League in 1901—to establish a two-league pattern that has remained fairly stable ever since.

Our memories of the early ballplayers are colored by their quaint uniforms, their decorative facial hair, and the poses they were forced to hold for several seconds while the studio photographer immortalized them. Yet they hardly deserve the condescending sneers of modern players and fans. George Wright, who earned $200 more a year than his brother, the first professional manager, covered more ground as a bare-handed shortstop than many a modern fielder with

This lithographed *Police Gazette* supplement gave ample testimony to the regard that professional players enjoyed in the 1890s.

his carefully designed glove. While his team was winning eighty straight games he batted .519, including fifty-nine home runs. That was his rookie year. In 1874 the Boston team won fifty-two and lost eighteen; so did its pitcher, Albert G. Spalding, who later switched from throwing to manufacturing baseballs. Adrian "Cap" Anson, one of the players who made the Chicago White Sox of the 1880s quite possibly the best team ever assembled, played major-league ball for twenty-seven years, topping .400 twice. When he was forty-six, playing his last season, his average dropped to .302. In a day when any pitcher with a lifetime total of 200 victories is considered an eighth wonder, we can only look back in awe at a lean moundsman who began throwing in 1890 and quit only after "winning pitcher" had been put after his name 511 times: Cy Young. Perhaps the oldtimers earned the right to chant:

> We used no mattress on our hands,
> No cage upon our face;
> We stood right up and caught the ball
> With courage and with grace.

Playing conditions were bound to change and, generally, for the better. Umpires were empowered to call balls and strikes. Catchers were provided with masks, chest protectors, and mitts and moved closer to the plate where they could take the pitch before it hit the ground. Pitchers were allowed to throw curves, if they could, and fielders were required to catch the ball on the fly and in their hands, instead of trapping it on one bounce in their caps. Different balls were tested. A lively variety produced one 201–11 score; a dead one led to a twenty-four inning scoreless tie. No happy medium has ever been reached, according to both pitchers and batters; but at least the scores became more reasonable and, by 1900, the modern era had arrived. Sports journalism ushered it in with gaudy and spacious coverage. Even while absorbed in building the war spirit against Spain, the New York *Journal* found a place on the first page, in red ink, for the up-to-the-minute line score of the local team's contest. By 1890 it was estimated that professional teams alone were drawing crowds of 60,000 daily, with semiprofessional and amateur games adding enormously and uncountably to the total. A true national sport had arrived.

Along with sports, the stage also profited from the growing degree of spectatorism. Competition for profits had produced a Great White Way of theaters in New York whose doors almost never closed. This was also the age of the promoters who, taking a cue from the successes of P. T. Barnum, set about to organize and publicize their properties. One manifestation of the profit urge was the "star system," which, contrary to popular opinion, was not invented by Hollywood but by producers who knew that anyone anywhere would pay to see Joseph Jefferson in *Rip Van Winkle,* and that it therefore mattered not one jot who played the other parts. The star and the producer made money from this arrangement at the esthetic cost of teaming talented actors with companies of second-raters. With theaters and opera houses appearing all over the country, the producer was also motivated to send a popular show on tour. Thus the road company, playing a single piece in different towns, replaced to some degree the repertoire company, which changed its offering without changing its location. James O'Neill, father of Eugene, found himself trapped by success in the title role of *The Count of Monte Cristo.* As the Count he broke out of prison and wreaked his ultimate revenge thousands of times in hundreds of cities and towns. In the more complicated business of arranging variety shows, booking agents eventually took control of performers and houses; and the sight of actors or performers stranded in Dubuque because of a misunderstood billing became rarer.

America had the audience, the buildings, and even the stars; but she did not yet have the playwrights. Serious theater, therefore, was almost exclusively a matter of imported operas and plays. Wallack's, Daly's, and Belasco's, the leading serious theaters of New York, featured eighteenth-century English, French, and German classics. For a while, actors like Adelaide Ristori, Fanny Janauschek, and Tommaso Salvini were encouraged to give these plays in their original tongues. The public eventually rejected the greater effort of following foreign dialog, text in hand, and only the opera continued to offer its wares untranslated. Their appetites whetted for serious music by the fabulous tour of Jenny Lind, "The Swedish Nightingale," Americans everywhere built opera houses and searched for able performers. Adelina Patti, a Madrid-born soprano, became the overwhelming favorite. Grand opera, however, was far surpassed by the vogue for Gilbert and Sullivan operettas, and particularly for "H.M.S. Pinafore."

Serious theater to most Americans meant intrigue, discovery, swordplay, gasping death, and exalted language. When the leading actor, pantalooned and cloaked, approached the footlights and took a careful three-quarter stance, hung his head and paused, the audience sat forward in their seats and rubbed their hands in anticipation. Next came the upflung arm, wrist leading the gesture to the final outward flowering of the gracefully cupped fingers.With this movement the head came back, the eyes went heavenward, the chest expanded, and the mouth opened with an explosive "O, what a rogue and peasant slave am I. . . ." In the balcony elbows nudged the ribs of neighbors as the spectators sighed, "Ah, now this is really it!'' No vehicles answered this need more aptly than the tragedies of William Shakespeare; no actor responded more ideally to popular criteria than Edwin Booth.

Son of an actor and well established by the time of the Civil War, Booth retired from the stage for several months after his brother's insane assassination of the President. When he returned to the stage the public, far from resenting Booth's kinship, seemed to feel that this family tragedy had

This portentous pose suggested the stylized interpretation, verging on melodrama, which made Edwin Booth as Hamlet the dramatic summit of the century. (Photograph about 1890)

heightened his ability to play the tragic figures of the drama. When he opened his own theater in 1869 with a production of *Romeo and Juliet,* tickets were scalped for as much as $125 each. At the height of his career, in 1887, he toured his Shakespearean repertoire with the assistance of another very able actor, Lawrence Barrett. Small towns from Oshkosh to Waco greeted the company at the train station and scarcely let them escape their adoring sight. In Kansas City the troupe played in an opera house so new the roof was unfinished; the shivering crowd gave them a doubly warming ovation. In the large cities they played to packed houses with ticket prices at least doubled by the fabulous demand. In spite of his great national popularity Booth, victimized by the star system, remained a controversial quantity among the acting immortals. His virtues went unchallenged in his own day, however, as witness his signal achievement of 100 consecutive performances of *Hamlet* in New York City, then as now a highly critical theatrical community. For those who saw it, Booth's portrayal of Shakespeare's puzzling, mind-torn prince provided a standard against which future thespians would have to prove themselves.

Unique to this era in its widespread popularity was melo-

All the tears and fears of the "Tom Show" were packed into this poster lithographed by W. J. Morgan, 1881. In some versions the ice actually moved on a rotary belt as Eliza fled the threatening hounds.

drama, with its coarsely drawn stereotyped villains, incorruptible heroes, and delectably pitiable maidens in distress. The taste for this genre seems to have sprung from the many successful stage versions of Harriet Beecher Stowe's sentimental novel, *Uncle Tom's Cabin*. Throughout this era "Tom Shows" toured the land playing in tents, on showboats, and in available theaters. Often a marching band paraded through town on the day of the performance, impressing the public with the troupe's ferocious leashed mastiffs. Complicated stagecraft was a partial key to *Uncle Tom's* success, the climax of the show coming either when the hounds chased the fleeing Eliza across the moving ice floes of the Ohio River or when Little Eva was literally borne aloft by ascending angels. The tone of these productions can be imagined from the stage directions provided by one such traveling company for the scene following Uncle Tom's death, played to the musical accompaniment of "Nearer My God to Thee":

Dark cloud drop rises slowly and discovers large fan C. [C, L, and R indicate stage center, left, and right] Fan separates from the C and falls slowly R & L—Discovering Tom on car, with back to audience and hands stretched upward. Two large silver and gold gates about 2nd grooves closed—on either side angels with large palms—Lights full up—Car with Tom accends slantingly upstage—The two angels swing around. Gates open slowly. Discovers two more angels R & L of track—Two angels are seated R & L on top of gate posts as car with Tom passes through the gates—back cloud rises and discovers Eva & St. Clare with angels extending hands to Uncle Tom. Green fire & c. Chorus of negroes all through.

Antislavery overtones forgotten, the *Uncle Tom* audience joined in an orgy of sentimental bathos, shuddering in horror at the brutal dogs, and gazing open-mouthed at the stage mechanics.

Producers of melodrama relied on heavy audience identification and participation. As villain they cast a man with fine aristocratic features and elegant mustache, costuming him in cape and top hat to establish his upper-class origins. The heroine was a plain but honest working girl; the hero, the sleeves of his workingman's shirt rolled up to reveal his brawny arms, bore the sometimes bewildered but always forthright expression of a child of the American masses. Augustin Daly, an American playwright who sometimes did better work, wrote the model melodrama for this era, *Under the Gaslight*. Second only to *Tom* in its popularity, this play originated the scene which was to become melodrama's true cliché: the hero tied to the railroad tracks, rescued by the heroine from under the very wheels of the pounding mail express. In another play, Daly had his hero tied to a sawmill log, thus creating the second most famous stock melodramatic scene as well. As with the "Tom Shows," other melodramas stressed tricky and elaborate stage mechanics and

The elaborate stagecraft, the moustached villain, and the hair's-breadth rescue guaranteed the success of the melodrama advertised in this poster. (Lithograph by H. C. Miner, 1897)

learned to produce some startlingly realistic effects. They were played as broadly as possible and invited audience response. A first-class villain could bring down the house with hisses merely by walking on stage; a poor one had to twirl his mustache. The exaggerated stylization of the performances hid what was often quite meager talent; for, as one reviewer probably quite justly wrote of a "Tom Show," the dogs were adequate but poorly supported by the rest of the cast.

The third category of popular theater would today be called the revue. Its earliest indigenous form was the minstrel show, which reached its height of popularity in the 1850s and stayed in the forefront of popular taste through the 1870s. Like the "Tom Shows" and the circus, it typically began with a parade, luring the spectators with fancy dance steps and popular airs. The singing and dancing on stage would be interrupted by comic exchanges between Mr. Interlocutor (the straight man) and the end men:

"Why is [Rev.] Henry Ward Beecher like Brigham Young?"
"Because he has married a great many women and keeps on marrying more!"

The minstrels were usually white performers in black face, although sometimes Negroes formed part of the troupe. The line was made up of singers and dancers who did specialty numbers during the "olio" part of the show. At the end of the line were the men who exchanged banter with the master of ceremonies.

E. P. Christy's Minstrels had the greatest impact because they introduced the songs Stephen Foster wrote especially for their shows, beginning with "Louisiana Belle" in the late '40s and continuing through "Old Black Joe" (1860). At least a dozen of Foster's songs remained on America's whistling lips through the Age of Enterprise and beyond. There were many other successful companies, however. Bryant's Minstrels played continuously to packed New York houses in the '70s, left for an eight-month San Francisco triumph, and returned to occupy their New York stage until 1890. As late as the 1882–83 season there were over thirty-two minstrel shows on the road; but their popularity was steadily giving way to vaudeville, a direct outgrowth of the minstrel variety segments with acrobatics, sleight of hand, and song-and-dance numbers. One difference was that, instead of making humor of Negro dialect and loose-jointed choreography, the vaudeville show made a mockery of all hyphenated Americans, especially the Irish and German immigrants.

Edward Harrigan, in the 1870s, began presenting shows at New York's Theatre Comique which parodied everything from baseball to politics. In later years he incorporated these sketches into farcical dramas like the *Mulligan Guards and the Skidmores* whose high point occurred when the Negro Skidmore lodge members fell through the floor of their meeting room and into the chambers occupied by the Irish Mulligans. All participants, attired in the full regalia of secret societies, clashed in a holocaust of comic uproar. With their thin veneers of continuity, these shows closely resembled many of today's musical comedies. The model for this kind of farce, with an unprecedented run of 650 performances, was Charles Hoyt's *A Trip to Chinatown,* in which temperance advocates and other sanctimonious reformers felt the barbs of Hoyt's mockery.

The difference between vaudeville and burlesque depended mainly on whether or not the show was intended for a mixed middle-class audience. The minstrel shows had begun to cross that line themselves. Emerson's Minstrels, Cincinnati's favorites, had to withdraw their slogan of "a new, chaste, and pleasing performance" after they were criticized for their "low moral tone." But it was the invasion of Lydia Thompson and her British Blondes, in 1869, coupled with the periodic revival of *The Black Crook,* an 1866 extravaganza, that convinced promoters of the money to be made by displaying scantily clad females in attractive postures alternated with sketches that were more earthy than witty. Burlesque had an older, respectable tradition of satire and parody, but after the British Blondes brought out standing-room-only signs across the nation, burlesque came to signify a deliberately bawdy style of humor and display, finally settling in theaters in the less respectable parts of town.

All over town, it would seem, the strains of music filled the late Victorian air. Organ grinders churned out Italian bel canto on downtown corners; from riverboat decks and amusement parks came the calliope's steam-powered toots of "Over the Waves" and other gay waltzes; and from the bandstands in the parks came the German style brass concerts, some as good as Patrick S. Gilmore and John Philip Sousa. Much of this music came from the stage, particularly the

The poor man's music hall. (Etching by G. Mercier after a painting, 1880.)

minstrel-born ballads of Stephen Foster and the perennially popular operetta arias of Gilbert and Sullivan: "Buttercup," "The Lord High Executioner," "Tit-Willow." Revues also left their audiences singing, and some of the most popular of the day's airs originated in musical comedies: songs like "Down Went McGinty," "The Sidewalks of New York," "The Mulligan Braves," and—the song that was adapted to carry the news of Corbett's win over Sullivan—"Throw Him Down, McCloskey." As the Broadway origins of these hits suggest, there was apparent by the 1890s a demand for new and plentiful popular songs which was answered by a "tin-pan alley" of composers. With the sale of three million phonograph records in 1900, popular music had become big business.

Popular songs were a lot more topical then than now. Dozens of titles were dedicated to the discovery of oil, the launching of the National League, the progress of women's dress reform—not to mention the various political campaigns and issues. When they were not being topical, the songwriters of the Gay Nineties were apt to be sad, moralistic, sentimental, and nostalgic. Paul Dresser cried in words and music for "the banks of the Wabash far away." Joe Stern asked his listeners to think of mothers and sisters who might need protection against the city's snares ("My Mother Was a Lady"). Jennie Lindsay warned, "Always take a mother's advice." A music that could be soulful and still make fun of itself—jazz—was on its way but. had not reached any considerable audience by the turn of the century. One of its precursors had begun to liven up the popular music front, as "My Gal Is a High Born Lady" and other tunes lent themselves to the fast-stepping, cluttered syncopation of ragtime.

Tin-pan Alley was by no means the whole musical score. The founding of institutions such as the New England Conservatory (1867), the Cincinnati College of Music (1878), and the Metropolitan Opera (1883) showed that Americans were taking serious music seriously. Theodore Thomas assembled a May Festival in Cincinnati in 1873 which became an annual and world-famous highlight of choral music. He then organized the Chicago Orchestra (1891), which took its place alongside the New York and Boston symphonies (1878, 1881) as aggregations which contributed to the national pride of Americans who took concert music as a hallmark of civilization. A few talented composers were gaining recognition beyond the ephemeral world of the popular song: Ethelbert Nevin ("The Rosary," "Narcissus") and Edward MacDowell ("To a Wild Rose") wrote tone poems and piano compositions which have endured. Meanwhile, nameless Americans everywhere were buying pianos and other musical instruments without restraint, subscribing for lessons for their children, and bursting into evening song whenever anyone struck the right chords. In 1900 over

$42,000,000 worth of musical instruments were manufactured for sale in the United States, a fourfold increase during a period when the population increased only two and a half times.

During that same period book publishing enjoyed an almost identical rate of growth, turning the century with an annual value of $44,300,000. Fiction was the most popular category, followed by religious works and children's books, but with a growing interest in books on history and government as the century neared its close. To meet this demand publishers competed wildly and often irresponsibly, tempted by the absence of firm international copyright laws before 1891. Mark Twain, for example, estimated that he was poorer by some $5,000 a year because of the Canadian publishers who pirated his books and sold them back into the United States. Celebrated European authors lost even more through the sale of unauthorized editions in this country.

Competition brought about a catering to some of the same tastes that produced the large-circulation periodicals. Pulp magazines, for example, had their exact counterparts in the dime and half-dime novels promoted by Erastus Beadle and his imitators. Stressing the lure of adventure wherever it was to be found, these tales made literary capital out of the frontier experience with such titles as *Deadly Eye,* and *Spitfire Saul, the King of the Rustlers.* Horatio Alger, who first made the best-seller lists in 1867 with *Ragged Dick,* appealed to the spirit of self-help and individual initiative on which so many educational and informative magazines were based. Books also reflected the rising importance of female tastes and interests. Not only did this interest produce a spate of cooking and home-management books, but it slanted the fiction market strongly toward the kind of sentimental romantic tale that women readers were supposed to prefer. A prime practitioner of this literary style, Mrs. E. D. E. N. Southworth, made a best-seller of *The Curse of Clifton* (1852) and continued through her sixty novels to enjoy as profitable a literary career as any American of her day. Her melodramatic romances, often set in the prewar South, usually appeared first as magazine serials and even thereafter sold hundreds of thousands of copies. In both 1863 and '64 she published two best-sellers in the same year. Louisa May Alcott's *Little Women*, a best-seller in 1868, remained a favorite with young lady readers throughout these years.

A mixture of sentiment and adventure accounted for the enormous American popularity of such European writers as Charles Dickens, Walter Scott, and Edward Bulwer-Lytton. Mystery tales grew in vogue from the isolated success of Wilkie Collins' *Moonstone* (1868) to the Sherlock Holmes mania which caught American readers in the 1890s just as surely as it did their English cousins. The advent of the yellow press, with its emphasis on the strange and the criminal, helps explain the popularity of both the crime tales of A. Conan Doyle and the science fiction of Jules Verne. The "muckraking" interest of the press in political and economic problems had a few counterparts among the books which sold well. Mark Twain's satire on Washington corruption, *The Gilded Age*, written with Dudley Warner, captured its share of readers in the 1870s. A rash of utopian romances in which an imaginary ideal society was contrasted with the flawed American present showed a mood of protest in the 1880s and '90s stimulated by Edward Bellamy's best-selling *Looking Backward 2000–1887*. Henry George, a journalist and economic theorist who ran for mayor of New York, attracted discontented readers by the thousands to his *Progress and Poverty* (1879).

The subject that dominated book publishing to a much greater extent than it did the periodical world was that of religion. Many of the sentimental novels, like those of Harriet Beecher Stowe which remained popular throughout this era, had a distinctly religious flavor. Historical novels found a sure market if they dealt with the early Christian period, as did Lew Wallace's *Ben Hur* (1880) and Henryk Sienkiewicz's *Quo Vadis* (1896), both permanent best-sellers. Application of Christian principles to contemporary living was the theme of the era's runaway leader in the sales parade: *In His Steps* (1893) by the Congregational minister Charles M. Sheldon. In his fictional exploration of one aspect of the social-gospel movement, Sheldon depicted the changes that came over the members of one church when they were persuaded to make personal decisions by answering the question, "What would Jesus do?" Estimates of this book's sales in the United States range from 2,000,000 to 8,000,000, with even greater sales abroad. "It is probable that there was never a year in American history in which the Bible did not excel the next-best seller," wrote Frank L. Mott. Preoccupation with religious questions was reflected in several of the Bible's closest competitors.

The taste for fiction that was either adventurous, sentimental, or religious—at best, all three—kept submerged most of the realistic and local-color writers whom today's literary historians regard as the important writers of the period. Mark Twain's tales of growing up along the Mississippi and Bret Harte's melodramatic yarns of the mining camps caught the immediate fancy of the reading public as well as the critical approval of the professors. Edward Eggleston's bitterly realistic *The Hoosier Schoolmaster* (1871) and Stephen Crane's authentically reconstructed story of a Civil War soldier's initiation to battle, *The Red Badge of Courage* (1895), were two lonely exceptions to the popular failure of the important pioneers in the realistic, naturalistic vein. James Whitcomb Riley, a folksy Indiana bard, was the only best-selling native poet who is at all remembered today.

Popular taste in painting and sculpture was probably even more an anathema to the critic than was the record of public preference in literature. The painters of that era who seem superior today—Winslow Homer, Thomas Eakins—were admired far less than the painters of enormous romantic landscapes and seascapes which sold by the square yard of canvas. Instead of the realism of an Eakins, most people preferred the unsubtly contrived lithographs of Currier & Ives which managed to make even urban industrial scenes seem bucolic, uncluttered, and nostalgic. To the classically exacting sculpture of William Rimmer and George Barnard they preferred the homely scenes of John Rogers, which told familiar stories. The crafts of engraving and lithography rose to a very high level in the second half of the nineteenth century, but they were sometimes appreciated for the wrong reasons. The "chromo," or chromolithograph, was the most popular single item of late Victorian interior decoration. Chromos by the million were given away as magazine subscription inducements; chromos by the dozens adorned the pages of calendars. The public admired them not for what they were, but because they were made to look like original oil paintings. Oliver Larkin, a historian of American art, found this an age which harbored a perverse interest in misused materials. Thus, one of the stellar attractions of the Philadelphia Centennial was a statue of the "Sleeping Iolanthe" made from fresh Arkansas butter and preserved within a framework of ice.

As subject matter for its art, the age preferred the great outdoors, particularly scenes of the towering Rockies, the giant sequoias, the crashing Western rivers, and the bottomless Grand Canyon. To hit the popular vein, the artist must have treated these subjects in a way to inspire awe and impress with grandeur. Objects of the new technology—particularly those that moved—were avidly pictured and tacked to home and office walls: gliding steamboats, pounding trains, and dashing fire engines. Scenes of disasters and their effects were painstakingly wrought and avidly sought: train wrecks, fires, floods, and earthquakes. Here, as in portraiture, the photograph gradually but surely replaced the lithograph and the chromo as an object suitable for framing. Faces of Civil War heroes, inventors, statesmen, authors, ministers, boxers,

HAVE YOU SEEN SMITH?

Much humor seemed directed at the embarrassment of certain groups, often ethnic or racial. This theater poster promised fun at the expense of police and the beach-costume regulations they were required to enforce. Contrast with today's bathing suits provides a third humorous dimension to this scene. (Lithograph by Strobridge, 1888)

JUST INSIDE THE LIMIT

and ballplayers stared out from available wall space. It seemed to matter little who the subject was, as long as he had an interesting—preferably bearded—face faithfully rendered by the artist or photographer.

Americans spent a good portion of their new leisure in trying to make each other laugh. From the stock of anecdotes carried by the drummer to the country store, to the carefully contrived humor of the newspaper cartoons and vaudeville skits, humor offered its eternal leaven to everyday life. One characteristic of the humor of the time was its use of obvious signposts. Cartoonists exaggerated the prominent features of their subjects and charicatured famous men mercilessly. Writers, to make sure their comic intent was understood, resorted to strange orthography. In the following passage Henry W. Shaw, as "Josh Billings," used the accepted pattern of comic spelling to philosophize about his subject:

> An Amerikan luvs tew laff, but he don't luv to make a bizzness ov it: he works, eats, and haw-haws on a canter.
> I guess the English hav more wit, and the Amerikans more humor.
> We haven't had time, yet, tew bile down our humor and git the wit out ov it.

Comical spelling was a close relative to the use of dialect; much of the humor of the age consisted in reproducing special dialects, both on stage and in print. Dialect was used, more often than not, to make fun of the group that was being mimicked. In fact the great common strain in Age of Enterprise humor was its tendency to deflate the elevated and to laugh at the expense of special groups.

Sport was made of politicians and presidents, Negroes and Jews, Catholics and Mormons, Irish and Germans, rubes and city-slickers, feminists and temperance advocates. David Ross Locke, writing under the name of Petroleum V. Nasby, produced an extremely bitter brand of humor:

> Wile Aberham Linkin wuz a livin, I need not say that I did not love him. Blessed with a mind uv no ordinary dimensions, endowed with all the goodness uv Washington, I alluz bleeved him to hev bin guilty uv all the crimes uv a Nero.
> No man in Noo Jersey laments his untimely death more than the undersined. I commenst weepin perfoosely the minit I diskivered a squad uv returned soljers coming round the corner, who wuz forcin constooshnel Dimekrats to hand out mornin.

Locke, whose Southern sympathies made him particularly

allergic to Lincoln, aimed a broad fire at politicians in general in a way that was more typical of his generation. For an honest political platform he suggested the following:

1st I want a offis
2nd I need a offis
3d A offis wood suit me; therefore
4th I shood like to hev a offis.

Palmer Cox, author of the popular "Brownie Books," reflected a representative kind of humor in his engagingly illustrated *Hans Von Pelter's Trip to Gotham,* wherein he ridiculed simultaneously the Dutch immigrant and the hayseed fresh off the farm. Hans, overwhelmed by the sights and sounds of the city, escaped being run down by the traffic only to have a crane accidentally pick him up and dump him in the river. In the museum he was arrested for jostling a statue; in the mill he was almost fatally ensnared in the machinery. Breathless with relief, he eventually made his escape to the rural community where his accent and unsophistication would not cause him pain and ridicule. In other sketches city dwellers were laughed at for shooting cows and snaring old shoes on their fishing poles, suffragettes were reviled for their manishness, and religious sects were lampooned for their unique tenets such as polygamy. Finley Peter Dunne, whose appeal as a literary humorist lasted well beyond the turn of the century, used the Irish immigrants who frequented Hennessy's Chicago saloon as oracles-in-dialect who saw through the pretenses of Andrew Carnegie, Theodore Roosevelt, and other celebrities. True to the conventions of victimization, however, Dunne sometimes made his characters turn on each other and, in the following passage, make fun of their own religion:

" 'Well,' says I, 'whin I was growin' up, half th' congregation heard mass with their prayer books tur-rned up-

side down, an' they were as pious as anny. Th' Apostles'
Creed niver was as con-vincin' to me afther I larned to
r-read it as it was when I cudden't read it, but believed
it.' "

The political cartoons of Thomas Nast, Homer Davenport, and others were sometimes truly savage in their animus.
The first comic strip was based on a series of cruel pranks
played on characters who spoke with German accents. The
pun, the tall story, the humorous twisting of new words and
ideas all persisted; but the surest way to make a nineteenth-
century American laugh was to find him a victim. If the man
who slipped on the banana peel hollered "Oops" in dialect,
so much the better.

Leisure in 1900 still included contemplative evenings on
the front-porch swing and drowsy afternoons on the living-
room divan; more and more, however, leisure meant going
out and doing things. Instead of sharing a glass of cider in
the kitchen with a caller, the man of the house would be
dropping down to the corner tavern or to the fancy men's
bars in the new hotels. Sometimes going out just meant sitting somewhere else, in a theater or a ballpark; but most
recreational hours were spent on the go. The extended weekend lent itself to trips—hiking, canoeing, cycling, and even
skiing. Boats and trains were arranged to accommodate
weekend schedules and even trolley cars were fitted out with
lights and brass bands to provide a summer evening of pleasant motion. At the dance halls and ballrooms activity was
almost as vigorous as at rural square dances. Waltzing couples created miniature V-shaped whirpools of dazzling turns
and glides; polkas , mazurkas, and schottisches sparkled with
quick, high-stepping movements; and Sousa's new "Washington Post" march turned dance floors into a coeducational
parade ground with the accelerated tempo of the "two-step."
To extend Josh Billings' remark, Americans took their leisure as well as their *haw-haws* at a canter.

Lithographed catalog cover, 1891.

6 The Age of the Periodical

BEFORE 1860 the country was sparsely settled, loosely connected, regionally divided, and not uniformly well educated. After 1920 the radio and the motion picture began to rival the printed page as sources of information and entertainment. But between the Civil War and World War I was a golden era for the printed page. Benefiting from technological advances and from the growth of population and literacy, magazines and newspapers played an irreplaceable role in a crucial marketing revolution while they entertained, informed, aroused, and abused a population confronted with many kinds of turbulence. Representing more viewpoints than there were sides to any question, these colorful, experimental, often meteoric publications arose, fought, merged, and died, almost with the tides. Although the rough weather they encountered was often of their own making, those journals which survived the storm enjoyed a period of unrivaled influence and exhibited an exuberant vitality as exciting as it was unsteady.

As a group, the periodicals of this era were neither overly modest nor unaware of their influence. The jauntiness of their tone can be judged from these words with which *Frank Leslie's Illustrated Newspaper,* a popular weekly then selling for $4 a year, opened its thirty-ninth volume in September, 1864:

Another volume opens with this number of . . . the most successful illustrated paper in the country, as its long career shows; for one after another the rivals which have risen have disappeared, after a brief and ineffectual attempt to compete with us in enterprise, tact and a full understanding of what the American public in their good taste require of any one who claims to instruct and interest them.

With a staff of special artists, whom long training has made unequalled, our facilities are almost incredible, and the truthfulness of our sketches makes the paper really one of the wonders of our time. . . . The corps of graceful American writers . . . contribute interesting tales . . . unrivalled in skill and power.

If boasting tempts the gods, then Leslie's paper should have failed forthwith; but such was not the case. The enterprise and understanding of the house of Leslie survived the wild spending of its owners and the death of its founder. With the corporation in the hands of the receivers, the widow changed her name legally to Frank Leslie and continued the management of nine highly successful publications which brought varyingly graceful and authentic news, features, and fiction to many homes. Well might *Leslie's,* and its comparably successful rivals, boast; for the periodical press of the age had unusual power as well as popularity. Collectively, the newspapers and magazines of the nation could claim to have defeated Presidents, started wars, cleaned up slums, promoted sports, and trained an entire generation of writers and artists.

This new and expanded power of the printed word was, in keeping with other new forms of power, based on new technology. A massive publications industry, to start with, needed masses of cheap paper. This need was answered, thanks to some observant Germans, with the discovery that paper could be made from wood pulp. By the 1880s, there were in America two successful processes employed in making pulp paper: the mechanical mashing and grinding of wood fibers, and the use of soda sulfite, or sulfate, to boil wood in chemical solution. Between them, they made a product durable enough to withstand high-speed printing and cheap enough to permit the penny press. For many printers Hoe's Lightning Press of the 1840s continued equal to their needs; but newspaper publishers, racing against time and competition, required even greater speed. Thus the Philadelphia *Ledger* happily installed William Bullock's web-perfecting press, which would accept a continuous roll of paper, print it on both sides, and cut the roll into pages. To Bullock's basic and, to those who watched it, miraculous process no important innovations were added; but capacity was continuously increased. The New York *Herald*'s electrically powered sextuple press installed in 1891 weighed fifty-eight tons and used twenty-six miles of paper in an hour, accepting newsprint from three five-foot rolls, folding and counting the papers as they came by the line. By 1900 even this capacity had been doubled.

When printing could be done at this speed, the bottleneck shifted to the process of composing and making up pages by hand. Charles Craske developed a technique for making casts of papier-mâché to receive the imprint of the type faces or plates, and then recast them in cylindrical shape to fit the printing surfaces of the new presses. Not only did this process save wear on the type faces and time for the compositor, but it also freed the printer from the tyranny of column widths. Formerly, his page was composed of parallel leaded columns, holding each other in place. With a page-sized precast matrix, however, he could make up his page from ingredients of any size he chose. Advertisers, if they wished, could mail these lightweight casts to any publication and insure themselves of a standard impression. A much greater economy of time was made possible by the invention of Ottmar Mergenthaler's "Linotype" first used by a newspaper in 1886. This machine brought an end to the laborious process of selecting type bars for each character from a job case, arranging them in a "stick," and then distributing them to their compartments when the printing had been done. Instead, the typesetter composed on a typewriter-like keyboard. The result was a complete line of type cast from molten metal, which had simply to be thrown back into the melting pot when the work had been completed. No single invention speeded up the printing process so much as this mechanical typesetter.

In the reproduction of visual materials another revolution took place. The first half of this revolution was in the transformation of photography from the cumbersome, time-consuming, expensive daguerreotype process which limited this art to the professional and limited his subjects to those that were practically immobile. Wet-plate, then dry-plate techniques marked the progress of the 1870s; with George Eastman in the '80s came the innovations—a flexible, quickly exposed rolled film mounted in a lightweight camera —which produced the Kodak and added photojournalism to the publisher's resources. The second half of the revolution was in the development of a printing technique which would do justice to photographs and, finally, to paintings and lithographs as well. The illustrated papers through the 1880s relied principally on a corps of craftsmen of whom publishers like Frank Leslie could be justly proud, since they often contributed more heavily to the final effect of visual materials

Advances in the craft of lithography and the introduction of rotary presses (one shown in background) were but two of the many technical aids to a great age of journalism. (Lithograph by L. Prang, 1874)

than did the original artist or photographer. But their skills were limited by the possibilities of line engraving, whether they used wood or metal for their plates. To pen or pencil sketches they could do nearly complete justice, depending on the complexity of the drawing; but to photographs, lithographs, and paintings, whose shadings were nonlinear, they could do only approximate justice. In 1880, however, Stephen H. Horgan introduced a process of photochemical engraving known as the halftone, which used tiny dots instead of lines to carry the ink, and which therefore could reproduce beyond detection by the naked eye the graded shadings which had made certain media resistant to the line engraver's skills. Photographs reproduced in this way were common enough by 1898 to give the American newspaper reader a camera's eye view of Manila and San Juan Hill.

Thanks principally to technology the publishing world, and particularly the newspaper world, had changed drastically since midcentury. Organized news services now gathered reports from all over the world and sent them by cable,

Advances in printing were matched by advances in literacy, particularly among women, as America became a nation of readers. (Photograph copyright J. W. Dunn, 1897)

telegraph, and telephone. Journalists composed their stories on typewriters and passed them along to composing rooms where the linotype cast them into metal. Together with the halftone plates, the type metal was recast in curved matrices for the cylindrical plates of the thundering presses whose rolls of pulp paper received the ink and then were cut, stacked, and folded into a whole city edition in less than an hour. By rapid transit they reached suburban homes. By fast mail trains and under reduced postage rates they reached their out-of-town readers quickly and cheaply. Everywhere they met an audience that was growing in literacy as well as numbers.

In price, size, and function newspapers and magazines were also transformed indirectly by technology. Inventions brought forth new and altered products. Mass production created goods in quantities which demanded national distribution. Many consumer items, under the new technology, had no real distinctions except their claims and their brand names. These conditions, against a background of improved transportation, distribution, packaging, and storage, placed a new stress on advertising. Billboards, considered unseemly by many, were the advertisers' only real alternative to the printed word; hence the periodicals felt the full brunt of a newly conceived industry which, while still in its birth pangs, changed the face and philosophy of publishing.

At the time of the Civil War, ads appeared regularly toward the back of magazines and toward the front of newspapers; a page of these ads resembled very much a page of classified advertising today, except for a number of small engraved cuts illustrating the pistol, watch, or artificial limb that was being sold. In spite of the garish claims of some vendors, the visual appearance of the page was dull and restrained. Inserts were normally limited to the width of a column and type faces were kept beneath modest size limits. The ads occupied a very few pages.

Soon, however, the pressure began to mount. Unverified figures suggest that in 1870 only about $20,000,000 was being spent on advertising in newspapers and magazines. By 1880 the figure was close to $40,000,000; by 1890, it had passed $70,000,000; and by 1900, in spite of the commercial depression of the 1890s, it had passed $90,000,000. In 1900 advertising was by no means the influential giant it had become by the 1920s, but it had gone well beyond the transmission of an unimaginative notice from a businessman to a newspaper office. Advertising agencies had been founded to serve as middlemen between the seller and the medium. J. Walter Thompson, whose agency first organized the placement of magazine advertising, invited clients in 1891:

> Advertisers who desire to avail themselves of my service in preparing advertisements, will please send me all their data, circulars, etc. I will then have the same prepared without cost . . .

Meanwhile, the Philadelphia firm of N. W. Ayer, which had been the first to control newspaper advertising for national products, had hired a full-time copywriter and artist. The inspiration of tradesmen and their agents had begun to

A NATIONAL DRINK

A HEALTHY DRINK

A FAMILY DRINK

A FRIENDLY DRINK

LAGER BIER

Ads like this could be cast from matrices with details filled in to suit a local situation; thus a common strain characterized printed ads across the nation. Note the German spelling of "beer" and the corpulent version of good health as opposed to today's accent on slimness. (Lithograph by Mensing & Stecher, 1879)

alter the appearance of the advertising pages as well as to increase their number. Instead of dreary descriptive texts, the readers of periodicals began to see sincere faces and sprightly slogans. Lydia E. Pinkham, whose Vegetable Compound was one of the many patent medicines which dominated advertising lineage, gazed with sympathy and assurance from periodical pages everywhere as she promised "a positive cure For all those Painful Complaints and Weaknesses so common among the Ladies of the World." Soaps, second only to patent medicines, made Victorian faces smile with recognition at the injunction to "Use Saplio" or the greeting, "Good Morning, have you used Pears' Soap?" Graphically, the hucksters of Ivory began to depict the terrible accidents that could be caused by treacherous soaps which sunk to the bottom of the tub. Instead of risking broken bones, why not

use a soap so pure that it floats? By the early 1890s Royal
Baking Powder had found its simple, insistent ad so profitable that it underwrote a $600,000 annual campaign for keep-
ing itself visible, and thus earned the reputation for having
the largest advertising budget in the world.

In the 1890s cereals first splashed their wares broadly
across the nation. A self-satisfied chef in his white hat held
out a steamy, inviting plate of Cream of Wheat. A rotund
Quaker, holding a scroll marked "Pure" in one hand, suggested the nutritional value of Quaker Oats. A vogue of
jingles was responsible for creating the short-lived but spectacular commercial success of "Force" cereal, manufactured
by Hornby Oats, and led to prominence by such rhymes as:

> Jim Dumps was a most unfriendly man,
> Who lived his life on the hermit plan.
> In his gloomy way he'd gone through life,
> And made the most of woe and strife,
> Till Force one day was served to him.
> Since then they've called him Sunny Jim.

Sunny Jim made more money than the Hornby Oats Company could manage successfully, but he proved the value of
an elaborate message trapped in a folksy format.

Two fads of the late century also colored the pages of the
journals. One was the new inexpensive camera which George
Eastman had ingeniously christened with a meaningless but
memorable name, Kodak. Boasting "You press the button;
we do the rest," the Eastman Kodak Company began its
relentless campaign to make the portable camera the inevitable hallmark of the traveling American. Bicycles, enjoying
their second great wave of popularity, vied for brand su-
premacy. The Pope Manufacturing Company, which eventually joined with another Hartford concern to make automobiles, advertised its Columbia bicycles as essential to
business and pleasure, and quoted one doctor as favoring

Great quantities of heavy material went into full-bustled fashions like these for winter afternoon wear in the 1870s. (Engraving, 187?)

bicycle riding as a superior prescription to "many a dry, formal medicinal one which I had to write on paper."

Shoes, trousers, shirts, collars, and all varieties of undergarments were nationally advertised, including Dr. Scott's Electric Corsets for Ladies and Gents which instilled vigor while they imparted grace. It was in local advertising, however, that wearing apparel led the advertising field, producing models of chatty salesmanship in the Wanamaker manner. Thus daily newspapers, as well as many family magazines, became by virtue of their ads virtual fashion magazines. The world of male fashion these ads displayed was not too remote from present-day men's apparel. The trousers were cuffless and full, the suit coats buttoned up to the clavicles, the ties were flat ascots, and the collars stiff, white, and three inches high. Bowlers and boaters were popular seasonally, and top hats were worn with much less provocation than is required today. Dandies affected checked trousers, floral waistcoats, heavy watch chains and cuff links; but a conservatively dressed fashionable male of the 1880s or '90s could have passed without much comment well into the next century.

With women's fashions, as always, change was the rule. The full skirts of midcentury were swept around in the "tie-back," and later the bustle appended a trailing shelf to the woman's waist. Strenuously laced whalebone corsets narrowed the waist itself to a waspish sixteen inches and created the silhouette of a tilted hourglass. Crazed with the possibilities of the new sewing machines, women burdened themselves with yards of embroidered decorations and pounds of unnecessary pleats and gores. Yet a countertrend was also at work, calling for simpler, more healthful fashion that would suit new generations of working girls whose frustrations with the old fashions were captured by Kathleen Norris:

> She wore a wide-brimmed hat that caught the breezes, a high choking collar of satin or linen, and a flaring gored skirt that swept the streets on all sides. Her full-sleeved shirt-waist had cuffs that were eternally getting dirty, her stock was always crushed and rumpled at the end of the day, and her skirt was a bitter trial. Its heavy brush binding had to be replaced every few weeks, for constant contact with the pavement reduced it to dirty fringe in no time at all. In wet weather the full skirt got soaked and icy. Even in fair weather its wearer had to bunch it in great folds and devote one hand to nothing else but the carrying of it.

As a result of this kind of protest, sheath skirts were introduced, at first disguised at the top by "fig leaf" aprons, but shortened to ankle-length for daytime wear. "Dress reform" undergarments protected female modesty without cutting off circulation. Sensible oxfords replaced pointed-toed, high-heeled pumps. The piles of real and artificial hair necessary to support in high fashion the modish pillbox hats gave way to less pretentious hair styles covered by broad-brimmed bonnets. Bodices and blouses, although they featured puffy leg-of-mutton sleeves and unnaturally broadened shoulders, were much less ornately adorned than were their high-fashion antecedents of a few years earlier.

The first effect of all this advertising was to increase the size of newspapers and magazines and to make them more expensive to produce. As a result, the publisher might easily have found it necessary to increase his price and to appeal to potential advertisers on the basis of quality: "It [*Arena*] reaches a wealthy constituency who can afford a five dollar magazine and who want and can buy what you offer." For a while advertising rates in the older, prestige journals remained high; but soon it became evident that circulation figures were to form the only important basis for advertising revenue. The increasing importance of this revenue forced on all publishers a kind of circulation war. The first weapon was price. Magazines worked their way down from the typical twenty-five cents to a dime and finally, in the great triumph of the *Saturday Evening Post,* to a nickel. By the 1890s all the great daily papers had lowered their price to two cents or a penny. The second weapon was the premium: the gift that came with a new or renewed subscription. The ridiculous extremes to which this device had been carried earned the scorn of a magazine which did not indulge in subscription lures; instead it advised a newly married man to furnish his home the easy way:

> By subscribing for the *Family Philosopher* he will obtain a commodious cookstove; a year's tolerance (paid in advance) of the *Prophylactic Prognosticator* will be rewarded by the gift of a black walnut bedstead; and the subscription price of the *Epizootic Essayist* will be returned

to him a hundred fold in the shape of a set of parlor furniture. . . .

Premiums gave way to group subscriptions and readers' contests as the circulation war went on. Sometimes the shooting became rather direct, as when William Randolph Hearst hired away his chief competitor's entire staff of premium feature writers and reporters, or, as in one Chicago newspaper battle, when organized gangs of pre-Capone enforcers were hired to intimidate rival newsboys and truckers.

Most publishers, however, relied on the content of their journals to win them the prize of readership. They made the most of new graphic techniques, using photographs, cartoons, and introducing comic strips. They kept up suspense-filled serial coverage of news events and issued serial adventure tales whose readers cried out in impatience for the next episode. They found or made lively issues in the events of the day. The pursuit of circulation, however, would be meaningless if, in the process, the publication offended the sensibilities of the advertising agent or his client. Since the price of many publications did not even pay for their distribution, let alone their manufacture, the publisher was forced to pay increasing attention to the interests of his advertisers. To some extent he censored the seller, refusing ads to some products and questioning the claims of others. But to a much greater extent, the advertiser was reaching a position whence he could exert great influence on what was written in any periodical that sought a profit.

With the lure of advertising income as an incentive, with an expanding urban population as a market, and with the technological tools to become fast, big, and flexible, American newspapers enjoyed a banner season at the end of the century. At the close of the Civil War there were about 500 dailies in the country with a total circulation of close to 2,000,000. In 1900 there were over 2,000 dailies (about 400 more than there are today) with a combined readership

One of the many great fires which plagued nineteenth-century cities and made headlines for journalists. (Lithograph by Currier & Ives of the Chicago fire of October 8, 1871)

of over 15,000,000. In 1892, if the claims of publishers can be believed, Boston's two largest papers sold a number of papers each day equal to three-fourths of the city's total population. In 1899, at the height of the foreign press, there were 773 German-language papers published regularly in the United States, 131 Scandinavian, and one each in Serbian, Armenian, and Japanese. Almost every crossroads had at least a weekly paper, and the large cities offered their residents the choice of a dozen dailies.

To modern eyes these papers, at least those published before the 1890s, would have a very subdued look. Heavy black type was used only in advertisements, and sparingly there. Stories, features, announcements, and small cuts marched down the large pages in regular column widths without calling typographical attention to themselves. Stories of routine local interest appeared side by side with calamitous news from Europe or Asia. Behind this plain façade, however, lay a morbid interest in the most minute details of tragedy which was no less lurid than that of the sensational presses of later years. There developed in these papers a style of reporting disasters—fires, earthquakes, train wrecks, floods, riots—that mixed sentimental observations with the most graphic kind of detailed reporting. The Johnstown Flood of 1889 furnished a good example.

One of the great disasters of the era, this spectacular flood was caused by the disintegration of a mountain dam, releasing to the already spring-swollen streams of the Conemaugh Valley a hurtling wall of water which suddenly buried the city of Johnstown, Pennsylvania, and the other settlements in that mountain basin. For almost two days all communication was cut off; then the stories began to come in. Here, on the first page of the Philadelphia *Press* of June 2, 1889, is a sample of the kind of coverage which readers had come to expect:

A Kurz & Allison lithograph of the era's most spectacular tragedy illustrated the morbid fascination with detail. (1890)

A NIGHT OF HORRORS
Thousands Dying Amid the Worst Terrors
of Flood and Fire
Special dispatch to THE PRESS

PITTSBURG, June 1.—Reliable railroad men engaged in the work of taking out dead bodies estimate that not less than 6000 people have perished in the series of disasters along the Conemaugh Valley.

Of all the fearful occurrences, the most terrible was the fire in which Supervisor Hayes, of the Pennsylvania Railroad, says, from 1000 to 2000 unfortunate beings were burned to death. The sight was so heartrending that the bravest men turned pale and sickened. Over 300 frame houses were jammed together in a heap forty feet high against the masiive [sic] viaduct of the Pennsylvania Railroad. At Johnstown all the houses were destroyed and the majority of the inmates crushed to death before the terrible fire began. Men, women and children, with their limbs pinioned between the timbers, their life blood slowly ebbing away, begged piteously for relief. One unfortunate woman asked a man on the bank for God's sake to cut her legs off. A man was caught by the arm and pleaded piteously for a knife to sever the member. Others were literally smashed and squeezed to death beneath the grinding timbers and surging waters. Some were pressed deep into the water and the flood soon ended their misery, but to add to the horror of this scene a fire broke out in the mass of timbers and nobody escaped. Flames soon devoured the people, and nothing now remains but charred and scattered remains floating somewhere on the water.

The repulsive fidelity of detail was not unique to this period, but the stamp of the age was clearly revealed in such maudlin phrases as: "begged piteously for relief," or "so heartrending that the bravest men turned pale and sickened." Carried away with sentimentality, reporters wrote in an exaggerated manner which today would produce only comic effects. This reporter, for example, left off his description of the fire to wander among the corpses, imagining what kind of lives the dead had led and how they had passed their final minutes. A smile on the face of one "poor, nameless woman," he wrote, "brought tears to the eyes of the rough men who found her. . . ." In this same paragraph he referred to the flood as an "awful mud-bedraggled, ghastly burden . . . that came in among the meadow." The precise spirit of melodramatic detail that colored so much of the disaster journalism, with its inevitable moral lessons of heroism and cowardice, could also be clearly seen in the engravings and lithographs which commemorated the same disasters.

Even more distinctive was a phenomenon called "yellow journalism" which originated in New York with Joseph Pulitzer's *World* and was deepened to its most intense hue in the circulation war between the *World* and William Randolph Hearst's *Journal* in the late 1890s. Taking its name from a daily cartoon character, "The Yellow Kid," who appeared in both papers after its originator was pirated from the *World* to the *Journal,* this kind of journalism introduced several features which are casually accepted today: the daily appearance of streamer headlines which cross the entire page; the lavish use of illustrations including cartoons and comic sequences; the development of multipage sports and women's sections as part of the daily paper; the emphasis on a large Sunday edition with numerous special sections and features, including a comic section printed in color. None of these innovations would have won these papers the readers and imitators they eventually attracted had it not been for an ingredient of sensationalism which has also remained as part of yellow journalism's legacy.

Scandals—personal, political, and business—claimed the consistent attention of this press. Some of these scandals gave birth to crusades for a less fraudulent New York City or a less monopolistic business structure and produced some important reform benefits. Too often, however, the scandals involved pointless personal tragedies—murders, suicides, perverted behavior. The *Journal* took a sadistic, pictorial interest in hunting trips and in a series of spectacles which pitted ring bulls against bears and lions. Next to animal cruelty yellow journalism favored science fiction and the occult. A real or supposed case of hypnotism made the headline on page three almost daily. A serial told of Thomas Edison's imaginary conquest of Mars. Drawings and tales probed the wildest possibilities of the future, the weirdest imaginings of the irrational mind, and the grossest nuggets of the nightmare past.

The pinnacle of yellow journalism was achieved by inflating one particular scandal: the treatment of Cubans by their Spanish governors. For years the American press had taken occasional and generally sympathetic notice of native uprisings. In 1895 a serious but short-lived insurgent plot reopened the issue. Misleading headlines ("Cuban Insurgents Win by Dashing Tactics") were accompanied by editorials accusing Spain of exploiting racial tensions in order to keep the island subdued. After the rebels were dispersed, the American interest in Cuba would doubtless have become passive again had it not been for the full-scale circulation war then reaching its climax between the *World* and the *Journal*. This competition led both papers into a frenzied campaign of headline-making: exaggerating the atrocities attributed to the Spanish General Valeriano "Butcher" Weyler, needling the leaders of Congress and the President for their caution, and building a mood of militaristic belligerence. The *Journal*, which had opposed McKinley in the election of 1896, was particularly virulent in its criticism of the President and Mark Hanna, the millionaire political boss who had helped put McKinley in office. This libelous attack reached its peak in a front page, two-inch banner headline: "HANNA vs. HONOR," blaming Hanna for America's failure to take a forceful line with Spain. The military might of Spain was given a detailed and, of course, unfavorable comparison with that of the United States. A talented group of cartoonists was put to the task of warmongering, showing an angry Uncle Sam eager to slay the Spanish vulture menacing the Cuban damsel, but restrained by a cowardly administration.

The ploy which showed yellow journalism in its most highly developed state concerned the insurrection president's niece, Evangeline Cisneros. Accompanying her father into political exile in the Isle of Pines, she was involved in an episode with the local military governor which ended in his being beaten and her being returned to a Havana prison. Miss Cisneros was accused of leading her captor into a trap where his assassination was attempted. The New York press preferred a version which had the governor assaulting the beautiful, helpless Evangelina and the natives springing to her defense. Now, wept the press, this innocent maiden whose only crime was to defend her honor had been locked up with the dregs of Havana. Hearst began a campaign of letter-writing in the girl's behalf, urging prominent Americans to petition the Pope and the Queen of Spain. When interest had been whipped to a fine passion Hearst sent to Havana a correspondent who rented the house next to Evangelina's prison, broke open a window, released the girl and smuggled her out of Havana disguised as a boy. As a grand climax Hearst also arranged a lavish public reception in New York and a trip to Washington where Miss Cisneros shook the President's hand. This episode showed the length to which papers pursued circulation stimulation. It was typical grist for the yellow journalism mill because it concerned the honor of a lady, because it had overtones of violence and sex, because it reflected evil on the Spaniards, and because it showed the paper to be a crusader in deeds as well as words.

With the sinking of the American battleship *Maine* in Havana harbor, the yellow press had all it needed to make a war. Heart-rending sketches and bloody word-pictures memorialized the infamous deed. A campaign was instantly begun to build a monument to the *Maine* dead. Although the cause of this disaster has never accurately been determined, the *Journal* unhesitatingly printed, on March 25, 1898, "SPAIN GUILTY!" in a banner three inches high, followed by the inevitable self-congratulatory "Evening Journal's Exclusive Forecast, Sunday, Confirmed by the President." With the opening of hostilities all papers sent platoons of correspondents and artists, setting up fleets of courier boats to relay news via Key West. The *Journal's* launch got so close to the fighting that a warning shot had to be fired across its bow; undaunted, Hearst himself led a shore party to capture a handful of Spanish sailors huddled on the beach. As the guns spoke, the *Journal* unfurled a new red, white and blue masthead of twin flags enfolding its revived motto: "An American Paper for the American People."

With the coming of the war, the two papers achieved their goal: a daily circulation of over 1,500,000. The cost of this achievement was no mean one. Many modern historians have joined with the alarmed E. L. Godkin in suggesting that without the prodding of the *Journal* and the *World* the war with Spain might well have been avoided:

Nothing so disgraceful as the behavior of these newspapers this week [mid-February, 1898] has been known in the history of American journalism. Gross misrepresentation of the facts, deliberate invention of tales calculated to excite the public, and wanton recklessness in the construction of headlines which even outdid these inventions, have combined to make the issues of the most widely circulated newspapers firebrands scattered broadcast throughout the country. . . . It is a crying shame that men work such mischief simply in order to sell more papers.

Hearst's days of mischief were not ended, however. His attacks on McKinley grew in vitriol as the campaign of 1900 approached. More than once his paper suggested that the only sure cure for the Presidential evil was assassination. When it was reported that McKinley's actual assassin had a copy of the *Journal* in his pocket at the time he fired the fatal shot, public resentment boomeranged to hit the publisher himself. Hearst was publicly condemned and hung in effigy; the circulation of his paper dropped sharply. In 1900 it was easy to see the influence of Hearst and Pulitzer spreading contagiously among the metropolitan press, but the turn of events in 1901 brought a dramatic close to the most spectacular aspects of yellow journalism.

Although some of the consequences of yellow journalism were grim indeed, it also left a legacy of humor which represented one of the most widespread and longlasting trends of the times. Comic drawings had appeared in journals for many years, but the weekly newspaper supplement stimulated an appetite which has proved almost insatiable. In 1897 a young artist recently employed by Hearst's *Journal* began a satire of famous German grotesque illustrations. As a center for the action he selected two mischievous brats, Hans and Fritz, who played a series of painful practical jokes on a gouty retired sea captain and his crony, the Inspector. As a series of panels which was repeated regularly with the same set of characters, Rudolph Dirks' invention, "The Katzenjammer Kids," qualified as the first comic strip. Other artists quickly followed suit until ten years later H. C. Fisher's "Mutt and Jeff" became the first comic strip to appear daily as well as Sunday.

This era also yielded the first bumper crop of columnists: men, and a few women, who wrote a regular essay wittily directed toward the day's most talked-about events and issues. For sustained quality over some twenty years, no one matched Eugene Field's "Sharps and Flats" in the Chicago *Daily News,* where he mingled verse and literary opinions with comments on politics and personalities. When President

Chester A. Arthur went west in 1883, for example, Field wrote a series of occasional verses which suggested the lightness of his humorous touch. One was a mournful complaint from the local Indians about the way the President had spoiled the fish with his fancy lures until they would no longer bite on humble bait. Another took the form of a mock heroic battle to save Mr. Arthur from kidnappers who turned out to be coyotes. A third paid tribute to Arthur's awesome courage in laying down a hand of five aces in a Yellowstone poker game and blandly hauling in the pot. From Mark Twain's Western tales, to Joel Chandler Harris' "Uncle Remus" legends of the Negro South, to George W. Peck's "Peck's Bad Boy" of Milwaukee, a rich menu of humorous dishes were served to newspaper readers throughout the country.

Magazines too served up some side-splitting stews, albeit sometimes too rich for the public digestion. *Phuniest of Awl* began publication auspiciously in New York in 1865, and ended unrepentingly while the calendar still showed that same year. Its nearest rival, *Phuniest of Phun,* also began in 1865, but survived well into 1866. The short careers of these two "phunsters" show something about the magazine world in the late nineteenth century. In the first place, new magazines were cropping up with the frequency of bad weather on weekends. In the second place, they did not last very long. Frank L. Mott, the historian of American periodicals, estimated the average life of American magazines after the Civil War to have been less than four years. In the twenty years following the war, 9,000 different magazines were printed; yet in no single year were there more than 3,300 in existence. In spite of the high casualty rate, however, magazine publishing maintained a general upswing, from about 700 titles in 1865 to about 5,500 in 1900. Furthermore, the idea of mass circulation, low price, and revenue through advertising had produced about a half dozen periodicals which had passed the 500,000 circulation mark by 1900, led by *Com-*

Colorful illustrated ads with typographic variety contrasted sharply with the bleak pages of newspapers and magazines only a decade earlier. (See page 181.) This lively 1900 page helps show why the *Ladies' Home Journal* became such a circulation leader.

fort, *Ladies' Home Journal, Hearthstone,* and *Munsey's Magazine.*

The near similarity of the comicly misspelled magazine titles of 1865 makes a third point about journals of this era: the fact that they covered all conceivable subjects and points of view. The *New England Farmer* was a publication just for that hardy Yankee, however shrinking may have been his number; another journal called *Wild Oats* had more to do with why farmers were leaving the farm. Arcane interests were represented in the *American Journal of Conchology,* the *Heraldic Journal,* and a San Francisco publication lasting only a year which was presumably for or about *Esquimaux.* Trade magazines, like the *Butcher's Advocate and Market Journal,* were founded in answer to special needs, and survive today. Even the *Horse Shoer's Journal* lasted until 1930. *Bonfort's Wine and Spirit Circular* served the merchandiser rather than the individual consumer, but the *Crockery and Glass Journal* showed the beginning of collectors' interests.

Men's clothes were made of heavy fabrics and, in their relative formality, emphasized class differences considerably more than is the case today. (See page 184.) This lithograph by Major & Knapp was made to announce spring and summer fashions for 1886 in New York.

Fads like cycling and croquet were abundantly covered in special periodicals, and almost every imaginable sport and hobby either had a magazine devoted to it or was about to. On the political front, seven different shades of socialism were available. It was possible to find manufacturers' magazines favoring the organization of labor and workingmen's magazines opposing minimum-wage and maximum-hour legislation. It would be hard to imagine a time in any nation's history when there were, per capita, so many magazines representing such a fever of activity on so many fronts.

If there was any one subject that particularly characterized this effervescent era it was the "woman question." With more education and leisure came increased purchasing power. Advertisers, with their emphasis on fashion, femininity, and fragrance, showed their complete awareness of this fact. Shrewd publishers of newspapers and general-interest magazines began to help their circulation by adding features on home management, social etiquette, and clothes design and by including sentimental romances in serial form. The distinguished intellectual journal *North American Review* printed an argument against women's suffrage by the famous historian Francis Parkman. It quickly came to its senses, however, by answering Parkman with a cooperative rebuttal from the pens of the nation's foremost suffrage advocates: Julia Ward Howe, Thomas Wentworth Higginson, Lucy Stone, Elizabeth Cady Stanton, and Wendell Phillips. Parkman was allowed an answer, but he was outweighed and outnumbered. A magazine might have a little mild fun at the expense of crusading women, but no circulation-conscious editor would dare place himself directly in the path of the feministic steam roller.

The force of the steam roller could be gauged from the uncompromising title of Susan B. Anthony's women's rights magazine founded in 1868. She called it *Revolution,* and under its masthead ran the motto: "The true republic.— Men, their rights and nothing more; Women, their rights and nothing less." When the torch of *Revolution* fell to the ground through financial difficulties in 1872, it was snatched up again by Mary Livermore and then by Lucy Stone in *Woman's Journal.* Meanwhile, two exceptional sisters were getting more publicity through their magazine than any amount of paid advertising could have earned them. Their names were Victoria Claflin Woodhull and Tennie C. [Tennessee] Claflin. Their *Woodhull & Claflin's Weekly* set Victorian America on its collective ear for a few years in the early 1870s. In compounding a journalistic point of view from equal parts of women's rights, spiritualism, and free love, these ladies had discovered the secret of offending nearly everyone. Particularly in their attacks on the double standard of sexual behavior for men and women, the *Weekly*'s editors spoke and wrote with such detailed candor that their contemporaries were always locking them up for obscenity. Beginning with the announcement of Victoria's

This Butterick Co. lithograph for the fall of 1891 showed the leg-of-mutton sleeve in ubiquitous triumph. The bustle had been subdued, the wasp waist relaxed a bit; but the only real simplification of attire was in the children's dresses. A version of the sheath skirt with "fig leaf" apron (see page 185) may be seen on the second figure from the right in the top row.

candidacy for the Presidency, reaching the high point in its career with its exposure of the extramarital relationship between the famous Reverend Henry Ward Beecher and the wife of his equally prominent friend, Theodore Tilton, the *Weekly* stood on the sensation-conscious fringe of feministic journalism and showed clearly what degrees of public interest could be attracted to this subject.

Of greater importance than the militant or sensational journals were those which reached out to women in the environment of their homes, educating them as tastemakers in the logistics of family life, and rendering them an active force for change in many domestic matters. The great women's magazine of midcentury, *Godey's Lady's Book,* captured its audience through its superbly detailed engravings of long-gowned and gusseted ladies, whose carefully tinted regalia made them suitable for framing as well as imitation. Along with the patterns for these dresses went a regular ration of sentimental fiction in which the main concern was whether the heroine was marrying beneath or above her station. This combination had produced a circulation over 100,000 by 1865, but from that point on its share of the women's magazine market began to slip. In the 1890s *Godey's* recognized that a "new woman" had arrived, and replaced the romantic tales with well-researched articles on topical matters; but this change of direction had come too late.

Godey's place had been permanently taken by a young immigrant named Edward Bok who, in 1889, succeeded Mrs. Cyrus H. K. Curtis as editor of the six-year-old *Ladies' Home Journal*. In a few years he raised this already successful magazine to the unheard-of million mark in monthly circulation. He did it by convincing the American woman that she ought to have a set of standards not only for clothing herself and her daughters, but also for furnishing and designing her house and for reacting to all she saw in her environment. Bok, whose zealous preference was for the straight line and the unadorned, lectured his readers on the virtues of rugged mission chairs and on the immorality of Queen Anne-style ornamented exteriors. To Bok taste was a crusade, and he made millions of American women his militant partners in opposing anything fancy, from Pullman cars to toilet sets. His great triumph came when he persuaded an anonymous architect to design for the *Journal* floor plans and specifications for a series of functional, parlorless homes to be built for less than $5,000. Although opposed at first by architects who thought he was taking away their business, Bok promoted his homes through contractors, developers, and speculators until whole communities of *"Journal* houses" stood as visible evidence of the breadth of his influence.

A look at the journalistic scene of the end of the century showed how distinctly women were emerging from their position as "the other sex" to a position at the center of social interest. Male and female writers in newspapers and maga-zines discussed whether woman was physiologically equal to the task of intellectual competition with man. The entrance of women into historically male professions was greeted with mixed amusement and admiration, but never with indiffer-ence. The New York *Journal,* for example, gave space to the selection of a female reporter to visit the Cuban insurgents. Its attitude toward this event was a curious mixture of re-spect for this courageous woman and amusement at the old-fashioned chivalry of the Spanish troops which would sup-posedly prevent them from executing a woman for doing what some male reporters had been shot for doing. Similarly, there was a continuous debate between those who thought of female dress as a statement of decorous idleness and those who thought that health and freedom of movement should be the determining fashion ingredients. Women were advised, sometimes contradictorily, how to behave in colleges and offices, where they were entering in ever-increasing numbers, worlds that had been dominantly male. In almost every phase of their lives, from dressing for a bicycle trip to entering politics, women were self-consciously reconsidering their role and status. The journals of the day gave them an abundant forum for their discussions.

Next to their preoccupation with the woman question the periodicals of the Age of Enterprise were most distinctive in their development of a school of journalism which Teddy Roosevelt eventually labled with the name that has stuck: muckraking. Like the man with the muckrake in *Pilgrim's Progress*, these writers looked not toward the heavens for things to praise, but toward the earth for the worst examples of things to condemn. Jacob Riis' articles on slum evils writ-ten for the New York *Sun* were preeminent models for muckrakers who sought flagrant examples of corruption in places of responsibility which had resulted in human deg-radation and injustice. Thomas Nast, the famous cartoonist,

Muckraking photographs like this literally helped get the muck cleared out of city streets. This incredible picture was taken by Jacob Riis in Varick Street, New York, about 1890. (Riis Collection, Museum of the City of New York) See also pages 131–38.

earned a place at the head of cartoon crusaders for his relentless exposure of the Tweed Ring and the malfeasances of Tammany Hall. When Hearst came east to New York he brought with him Homer Davenport, who not only incited a nation to hatred for Spain but also stabbed with his sketching pencil the monster trusts and other targets of public resentment. In the 1890s magazines like *Arena* and *Forum* began to make exposure a regular item in their tables of contents, and *Puck* was running a two-page colored center spread by Joseph Keppler accompanying a biting exposé.

Muckraking as a journalistic movement reached its climax in the first decade of the twentieth century, but it was well grounded in the protest journalism of the 1880s and '90s. "Two Weeks in Department Stores" was by no means as sensational in its rhetoric and subject matter as Jacob Riis' slum scenes, but it showed how widespread was the muckraking viewpoint by 1899 when it appeared in the *American Sociological Review*. Almost without pausing to argue, the

Having helped Hearst whip up war spirit, cartoonist Homer Davenport turned on the trusts, which he personified in this neolithic monster. The caption read: "This is the day for little people. Will they do it?" (Pen-and-ink drawing, about 1900)

author assumed that evils exist to be exposed, preferably from the inside:

> The necessity for a thorough investigation of the work of women and children in the large department stores in the city was apparent, and the difficulties manifold. . . . It seemed evident that valuable information could be obtained if someone were willing to endure the hardships of the saleswoman's life, and from personal experience be able to pass judgment upon observed conditions.

Annie MacLean gave up her middle-class comforts for a period of two entire weeks while she lived in a boarding house with immigrant girls and shared their lot as department-store salesgirls. She discovered how abusive customers and employers could be, how difficult it was to earn more than mere subsistence, and thus how tempting it became for working girls to sacrifice virtue for the sake of economic opportunity. Poor food, unsanitary facilities, and long hours compounded the problems she observed. After completing her catalog of abuses, she took the muckraker's second step in assuming that something could be done about these abuses:

> Women and children are in the industrial world . . . and as the weaker members of society they need protection. Inhuman and demoralizing conditions must be removed.

She ended her article by recommending legislation, inspection, and a consumers' boycott of stores which did not treat their employees properly.

Tutored by their journalists, Americans had begun to see that the new urban industrial life under the hegemony of professional politicians and trust tycoons was not without its seamy side. They developed an appetite for the most appallingly detailed and authenticated exposures of these conditions which they followed with an energetic commitment to "do something about it." Americans, as seen through the welter and variety of their busy periodicals, were restless and excited. They could not get enough of new ideas like evolution. They were willing to listen to what Thomas Edison had to say about practically anything. They enjoyed their short, end-of-the-century war with Spain and the one-sided heroics of Dewey and the Rough Riders. They reveled in all their new toys: express trains and baseballs, bicycles and telephones. In spite of droughts and depressions they were cheerful and optimistic. Life was a romantic adventure, they seemed to say, as they devoured the pulp magazines with their precocious boy-detectives and their superannuated Buffalo Bills. In this adventure the prizes went to those who helped themselves; so they let Horatio Alger explain to them how an unschooled rail-splitter could become President of the United States and then they went out and bought self-culture journals or took correspondence courses.

By the end of this era the Civil War, with all its painful tensions, was well in the background. Its legacy of minority problems was momentarily forgotten. Instead, in the foreground was an easy victory by a reunited nation over a once-proud European empire which had financed the very discovery of this land. The Stars and Stripes was flying in Manila, Honolulu, and Puerto Rico. The elevated trains were rattling through the city skies and the automobiles had begun to frighten horses on country lanes. Evolution, most people seemed to think, meant that democracy and technology were creating the opportunity for an unprecedented paradise in America. With strenuous application of the energy of free men, Americans would get there; and when they did they would find that a magazine had predicted the date, a cartoonist satirized their efforts, and a newspaper reporter was already there waiting to interview them.

Here the cartoonist Joseph Keppler self-conciously highlighted the role of the press in exposing corruption, this time in the U. S. Senate. This scene makes a good visual definition of the term "muckraking": throwing the spotlight on wrongdoing. (Lithograph from a cartoon in *Puck,* 1890)

Halftone after painting by F. Cresson Schell in *Harper's Weekly*, August 1, 1896.

7 Urban Home and Family: 1890s

THE CENSUS OF 1900 showed half again as many people living in what demographers call "rural territory" as opposed to "urban territory"; but the shift from small to large communities was the prime feature of population change in the last decades of the nineteenth century. Between 1870 and 1900 the number of people living in towns of 2,500 to 3,000 increased by fewer than 2,000,000, while the number of people living in cities of over 500,000 grew by 6,500,000. In selecting a home and family to represent the changes that had taken place in everyday life since the 1860s, we can reflect the motion of the times by situating the 1890s family in the city. To be geographically representative this family would live somewhere near Columbus, Indiana, the approximate center of population in 1900, although most of the large cities were in the northeastern part of the United States. A family located in an Eastern city would be, if anything, farther from the mythical center of

American life than the smalltown family described in Chapter One; yet their home and their life in it can be taken not merely as representative of many Americans but as indicative of the more noticeable changes in domestic life.

Identifying the home of this family would not be nearly so simple as in the small town of the 1860s; for, as the century wore on, the variety of housing available to middle-class families increased. In an earlier day, the family would have had a rather straightforward choice between a home on the fringes of the city and a boarding house closer to the center of town in which they would share facilities—including the dinner table—with the other families in residence. Some boarding houses became famous because of the cuisine or the conversation of the proprietress. Others developed a reputation as a home for literary, theatrical, or political personages. Because a woman boarder was relieved of most household chores, however, the boarding house was criticized as a den of idleness; too-easy friendships acquired in such an environment were warned against; and the responsible magazines of the day conducted campaigns against boarding as a family way of life.

The home a family might have chosen on the fringes of an 1865 city would by the 1890s have been overrun by the city's expansion and become the site of a factory, school, or shop. The New York City of the '60s was confined politically to Manhattan Island and was densely settled only south of Central Park. By 1900 its legal boundaries had spread to include Staten Island, Brooklyn, all of the Bronx and part of Queens County, and its population had spread even farther. There was always, of course, the option of moving to a more remote residential area, an option made more appealing by the development of the electric railway, which encouraged the rise of suburbs. By 1895 there were 850 urban railway lines in operation, and it was a rare city that had not produced at least one satellite suburb whose breadwinners boarded the interurban trolley each weekday morning. Both by necessity and intent, life in these suburbs resembled more closely the small-town living of an earlier day than it did the bustle of the exploding metropolis.

Alternatives to boarding and commuting existed in the apartment and the row house. With the development of utilities and services, builders began to answer the demand for family living quarters in an urban environment by constructing six- or eight-story buildings in the heart of town. Modeled at first on the luxury hotels, they were called "French flats" and appealed to such men of means as the publisher George P. Putnam, who, in 1870, moved into an Eighteenth Street building designed by the famous architect Richard M. Hunt, and reputed to have been the first apartment house in New York. Soon there were enough such buildings to put them within the range of the middle class. For $75 a month a tenant could expect eight rooms and a bath, elevator service, a built-in kitchen range and a hot-water heater.

The row house, however, was a still more popular compromise in most cities. It satisfied the great American urge to own one's home, it segregated family activity on several floors, and yet it shared its side walls with its neighbors and sacrificed its surrounding grounds to the city's rage for space. Because they were economical not only to construct but also to heat and maintain, row houses had existed for centuries. In American cities, however, they were built with special fervor in the late nineteenth and early twentieth centuries and gave to certain neighborhoods a flavor which has persisted in spite of their deterioration into multiple-family dwellings or their equally ravaging "restoration" by real-estate promoters. New Yorkers knowingly refer to the "brownstone blocks" where row houses with reddish-brown sandstone façades began to appear in this era; travelers know they are passing through Baltimore when they see the bright red ranks of brick homes with white marble steps scrubbed each morning by a meticulous *hausfrau;* much of the varie-

This Easter-morning scene on Fifth Avenue in the 1890s showed the finest togs and equipages as well as a block of well-to-do houses. (Photograph by Detroit Publishing Co.)

gated gracelessness of Washington's Capitol Hill came from the miscellaneous row houses of the 1890s; and Philadelphia grew so addicted to the row houses that her citizens demanded them even in the remote suburbs. For a representative urban family dwelling of the '90s the row house would be a reasonable choice.

Although the wealthy favored horse-drawn landaus and phaetons with carefully polished veneers, the middle-class mode of arriving at the row house would doubtless have been by trolley or cable car. In a few cities the elevated railway might have served, and in Boston after 1897 America's first subway offered still another alternative. Although too far from the city's central train depot to be approached on foot, the typical row house would have been well within the network of public transportation, and the visitor's main worry would be the violent and unregulated streams of traffic that crowded the streets of these cities day and night. Yet this journey might well have been smoothed by the new asphalt

and brick pavements that were replacing the uneven wood-
and granite-block streets of midcentury.

Turning into the residential side street, we would be
greeted by a prospect that compared rather starkly with the
leafy quiet of a small-town residential neighborhood. Although some sporadic efforts were made to keep American
cities green, the progressive urge to pave streets and sidewalks typically won out. Instead of a row of elms or maples,
we would see a forest of utility poles, heavily laden with the
many wires then required to do the work of a single modern
cable, whose long electric branches touched at every house.
A cast-iron fence in front of the house might be the only
exterior reminder of the 1860s visit, and, having passed
through its gate, we would find ourselves standing in a tiny
front yard, entirely paved or else supporting only enough
grass or shrubbery to cover a standard billiard table. Just
behind the fence a large iron lid, circled by black tracings,
showed where the coal was taken in. Straight ahead a short
flight of stone steps led either to a small porch or, more
likely, directly to the main and sometimes sole public entrance.

Looking up we would see a relatively plain façade of
brick, limestone, or sandstone. Perhaps a bay window relieved the flatness of one or two stories. Perhaps the roof line
reflected a subdued classic shape or a pattern of ornamental
tiles. The use of multicolored brick enlivened some rows, and
intricate bonds, or ways of laying the bricks, added textural
depth to others. The only ornate or pretentious feature, usually, was the carved or milled oak front door set in a frame of
scaled-down half columns, and bordered at the sides and
above by panes of beveled, leaded, and perhaps tinted glass.
This doorway led not to a hallway but to a foyer designed as
a buffer between the precious centrally heated interior air
and the inclemency of the outdoors. Floored in white glazed
tile, the foyer had as its only furniture a large exotic urn
whose function was to swallow umbrellas and stand guard

over the wet footgear that might be ranged alongside it. From this vestibule an inner door of curtained glass set in a simple frame gave access to the hallway and staircase which occupied one side of the interior, from top to bottom. Off this hallway, in the manner of railway compartments, opened the various rooms, each of which—through ingenious setbacks, bays, and air shafts—offered some degree of outside lighting.

As the façades of these houses would suggest, the builder of 1900 had considerably more choice of materials and techniques than his post-Civil War predecessor. To dig his foundation he would hire a steam shovel instead of a horse-drawn slip scraper and thus save three weeks' time. If he had trouble establishing footings, he could bring into play a pile driver, patented in 1883, and avoid the arduous hammering with weights lifted by horsepower. Instead of walling the basement in stone, he could use the new Portland cement whose American patent holder, David O. Saylor, had won the highest award at the Centennial in 1876; or, if he were really up to date, he could use the structural hollow tile being developed in New York by Balthasar Kreischer. Chances are that he would rest his structure on wooden timbers; but, since the Homestead steel works of Andrew Carnegie began manufacturing them in the 1880s, he would have the option of using steel beams made expressly for building purposes.

In building a home in the 1860s the carpenter was boss and had only to accommodate the stonemason, who laid the foundation and built the fireplaces and chimneys. By 1900 this idyllic simplicity had given way to a condition much closer to the dilemma of the modern builder who must cope with and coordinate the problems and skills of dozens of specialists who equip the home for heat and light, water and sewer. Each of these specialists increased the range of choice: the kind of lighting, the style of fixtures, the type of furnace, the location of the registers or radiators. New floor coverings, such as linoleum, added to the variety of interior finishes; and the adaptation of power hoists and cranes to building purposes made it practical to think of stone walls and tile roofs instead of the almost inevitable frame, brick, and shingle exteriors of earlier days.

Row-house floor plans differed in many details, but their basic character depended on the use made of the basement. An early tendency was to provide a front basement entry, a half-flight down from street level, which was used by tradespeople and servants. Servants' quarters might occupy the front half of this floor; in the rear the kitchen connected by a dumbwaiter with the dining room immediately overhead. Two forces had begun to exert pressure against this arrangement. In the first place, as central heating became more common, space had to be found in the basement for furnaces, boilers, and coal bins. Then, as servants became less available and the housewife herself began to spend more of her time in the kitchen, a natural feeling arose for a first-floor kitchen with better light, ventilation, and greater convenience.

However the basement were arranged, it would offer the most direct evidence of changes in American homes—most obviously, the furnace. Although many homes continued to depend on stoves and fireplaces, the city dweller by 1900 had a wide choice of central-heating systems based on hot air, hot water, steam, or combinations of these elements. The earliest furnaces were simply large stoves surrounded by brick shells which admitted cold air through a grate at floor level, warmed it, and allowed it to pass upward through enormous pipes to floor registers above. The dry and dusty air emitted from these registers was not healthful, and the system did not provide a scientifically sound or technologically efficient method of distributing heat throughout the house. A process for making cast-iron radiators, developed in the 1890s, allowed for the widespread adoption of hot water and steam heat; but the ungainly octopus of a gravity-flow warm-air heating system continued to monopolize the basements and send its cylindrical tentacles squeezing through the walls and floors of many a late-century dwelling. Whatever the medium for distributing heat, the fuel remained coal; and the dusty coal bin claimed its inevitable place below the ground.

In further contrast to the home of the 1860s would be the welter of cast-iron, lead, and tile pipes, large and small, which clung to the basement walls and hung from the floor joists overhead. The smallest and most abundant of these pipes were those that connected to an outside gas main and carried its contents to hot-water tanks in kitchen and bathroom, to the kitchen stove, and to lighting fixtures throughout the house. Kerosene was the prevalent source of light in the 1860s and probably would have remained so until the coming of the Edison electric bulb had it not been for two developments of the '70s and '80s. The first was the discovery of T. S. C. Lowe that by decomposing steam and mixing it with gases and carbonic acid he could manufacture a highly efficient illuminant. This product, when burned in the conical mantles invented by Carl von Welsbach of Vienna in 1885, gave off a bright, steady light superior to any other available source. "Water gas," as the product was called, along with the Welsbach mantle, gave gas lighting a new lease on life, and made "The Gaslight Era" a phrase which still evokes the years around 1900.

The 1880s were the years during which most American cities began to tackle the problem of a public water supply; and, although they had by no means solved the problems of filtration and purification, it is quite likely that the urban home of the 1890s would have a second network of pipes to carry water from the city main to the bathroom and kitchen. The practice of passing the water through a basement tank and feeding a separate system of hot-water pipes was not common except in the first-class hotels and the homes of the wealthy; but it was possible to find small gas hot-water heaters in the kitchens and bathrooms of this era. Public sewerage systems lagged behind the provision of water; the typical

The photo was captioned "What artistic taste and refinement can do in an Alaskan cabin." In fact, this interior makes a good parody on the Ruskinesque emphasis on home-crafted objects and native materials (the pelts) and on the general clutter of late Victorian décor. (Photograph by B. Kinne, 1903)

home of the 1890s would have pipes draining sinks and water closets which led not to a sewer beneath the streets but to a vault beneath the back yard where waste materials were disposed of by means of cesspools or septic tanks. The residue was collected and, all too often, dumped into the nearest large body of water.

Ascending from the cellar we would find ourselves in the long side hall already glimpsed through the main entrance. Regardless of which of the many doors we opened, we would be likely to find a room carefully furnished and decorated as part of an overall plan. Once past the showplace of a parlor the post-Civil War house would have appeared casual and uncoordinated. The housewife of 1900, however, educated by the enlightened new magazines, would have been much more self-conscious about what was appropriate for each of her rooms and would have sought a degree of consistent style throughout. *Ladies' Home Journal*, first published in 1883,

The Turkish motif provided an excuse in this room for a surfeit of pillows and an endless echoing of the curvilinear designs of the art nouveau. (Photograph by George C. Boldt, 1902)

ran contests for the best furnished rooms of all kinds and photographed the winning entries. *Home Decoration,* begun in 1886, filled its pages with elaborate sketches of outstanding decor as well as detailed renderings of chairs, moldings, and wall panels.

The modishness of the era took several forms. There was the "cottage style," first popularized by Mrs. Sarah Joseph Hale, editor of *Godey's Lady's Book,* and manifested mainly in the spool-turned beds and couches of the period. Later this phrase became associated with John Ruskin's English emphasis on home-crafted rusticity. Mission style reverted to vague Spanish origins and stressed broad flat surfaces joined obliquely rather than at right angles. Also popular was a mildly Oriental atmosphere achieved through the use of rice paper, beaded curtains, and hangings of Chinese or Japanese mood. Except for the stolid dark woods of the mission style, the direction of this influence was toward a light and colorful effect. Particularly in row houses where windows were scarce, the housewife was reminded that curtains and drapes should be chosen so as to filter rather than to block the outside light. Plain white muslin, with a ruffled edge, was recommended as a window covering for those who preferred not to spend fifty cents for a roller shade; and the deeply swagged and festooned maroon and dark blue brocades and velours of midcentury were frowned upon. Over her hardwood floors the housewife was urged to place Canton or Japanese matting of neutral tones instead of the weighty and ornate carpets favored in the parlors of the 1860s.

In fact the very existence of the parlor had been threatened. Many floor plans still called for parlors, and a domestic-science book described the parlorless home as poor indeed; but the *Ladies' Home Journal,* in advising a new homeowner on furnishings in 1900, did not even mention a parlor. The description of the living room made it clear that this widely accepted source of good domestic taste had decreed forthrightly against the parlor and all the associations it once held:

> The living-room ought to be the most attractive place in the house. All of the furnishings should be of the most substantial and comfortable kind, with nothing too good for use, and nothing that will be harmed by exposure to sun and light. There should be a large table, a couch, a bookcase, some good pictures, good lights, and comfortable easy-chairs, in this room.

These furnishings were considered minimal, and one should by no means assume that an 1890s living room was austere or uncluttered.

A painted or plainly papered ceiling joined the quiet matting in providing an unobtrusive framing for this room, but in between was considerable visual activity. Walls were papered in lively floral patterns or in sweeping, intricate Ruskinesque curves. Instead of ceiling moldings there might be wood-outlined panels framing involved tapestries, curvilinear abstractions, or pastel scenes. The most stylish hangings would have included wispy reproductions of the determinedly romantic works of the English Pre-Raphaelites, or the boldly outlined, heavily bordered, and carefully balanced early products of a school to be known as the "art nouveau." Furniture upholstered in gay patterns mixed freely with wicker chairs and squarish wooden couches. Distinctive of this era was a variety of high-silhouette wooden furniture that always managed to look either Egyptian or medieval. Easy chairs were designed with the arms and back the same height, with the interior seat and back upholstered to match the wall paper. The arms and backs of small chairs were extended upward to enclose a clock at the top. Couches were enclosed on three sides and became bookshelves as they rose above head level. Window seats combined storage space beneath with high ends for backrests, and even dining-room tables were designed with headboards and footboards like a bed. Much of this fashion was due to the efforts of the English architect Charles L. Eastlake to revive the square, sturdy lines of Jacobean furniture with its restrained carving and handsome inlays of gold and lighter woods. His own pieces, displayed at the 1876 Centennial, produced a market for this style which manufacturers were quick to exploit, with the result that less sturdy and more ornate pieces of "American Eastlake" found places in many living rooms of the 1880s and '90s.

From the ceiling hung the brass fixture whose thin arms swept down and out in predictable curves, ending in gas jets half enclosed in opaque white shades. If the home were truly stylish, this fixture might have been replaced by one hung on heavy chains and ending in a multisided angular glass shade stained pastel colors and joined by metal strips. If there were no such chandelier, there might at least be a table lamp of this Tiffany glass, another product of the Ruskin revolution against mass-produced objects, whose maker took pains to design each item individually and to tint his glass so as to produce a deliberate exotic effect. "Burmese glass," his most popular creation, was a shading graded from salmon pink to lemon yellow. A room with a squarish window seat, a Tiffany lamp on an octagonal walnut table, and squiggly pastel wallpaper would need only one other attribute to identify it as typical of the Nineties: pillows. Even more than in the mid-Victorian parlor they occupied every horizontal space and added to the variety of shapes and colors. Women's magazines filled their pages with new designs for them, and women obediently filled their living rooms with them: flat ones and round ones, fringed and tufted ones, pillows made of cigar bands, autographed pillows, pillows with Greek letters sewn on, ruffled pillows with pink and black checkerboard centers, blue denim pillows embroidered with the music for a Wellesley college song, hexagonal patchwork pillows with raised squares of all the colors in the housewife's sewing bag.

If we escaped the living room without stumbling over a

A *Journal* contest in 1900 produced these winners.

THE LADIES' HOME JOURNAL

A DOZEN GOOD SOFA-PILLOWS

From Photographs Submitted to the Journal in Prize Competition

fallen pillow, banging an elbow on the angular furniture, or
nicking a temple on the low-hanging lamp, we would find
ourselves in a dining room which had changed very little in
the last thirty years. Wall coverings and hangings would attempt to carry on the living-room decor; but, unless the
homeowner had gone overboard for one of those hand-
crafted tables that looked like a bed, we would see the same
oak or mahogany table, chairs, sideboard, and china cabinet
that we saw in the 1860s. The design might be simpler and
more stylized, but the same dark woods would give forth the
same assurances of sturdiness and the same promises of linen-
crystal-silver magnificence before a holiday spread. A somewhat smaller table would be required, and the entire furnishing, including carving set, table linen, china, glass, plated
silver, window shades, and nine yards of matting for the
floor, could have been purchased for $164.50.

Either behind or beneath the dining room would be found
the pantry and kitchen, floored with either tile or linoleum
and provided with more built-in closets and cabinets than
would have been the case a generation earlier. In addition to
storage cabinets for food and dishes, the pantry would have
contained something called a refrigerator which, as the tell-
tale drip pan underneath revealed, was only a slightly larger
and more efficient version of the icebox. Artificial ice and
mechanical refrigeration had both been invented by this
time, but these inventions had not yet been applied to the
preservation of foods in stores and in homes. The kitchen, in
fact, tended to show a lack of confidence in the technological
revolution that had taken place in the last decades. Although
the room would be lit by gas or electricity, it still had a shelf
on which were ranged a row of kerosene lamps, cleaned and
ready for the moment the lighting failed. Likewise the stove,
although supplied with gas burners, still reflected the cumbersome design of the coal- and wood-burners and was often
in fact a "combination stove" in which a fire could be built if
the gas were not functioning. This black iron monster still

dominated the room; notable changes could be observed in the sink, with its hot- and cold-water spigots and sewer-pipe outlet, and in the proliferation of mass-produced metal utensils: beaters, slicers, grinders, mashers, and measurers. This wealth of tools, added to the greater variety of produce, tended to clutter kitchens that had been designed in simpler days; hence cabinetmakers bent their efforts to solve the problems of kitchen management by providing complex storage units with bins and boards, sliding shelves and drawers. The disappearance of the coal and water pails from their place beside the back door offered an absent testimony to the advancing ease of housework.

If the kitchen were in the basement, the first floor might have an additional room: an old-fashioned parlor, or a more modern den or library. Ornamented fireplaces were still popular in such rooms, and the style of the mantel or facing might be used to set the tone for a decorating scheme. A den would still include a rolltop desk flanked now by a Morris chair. Any room could become a library with the newly popular sectional bookcases, glass-fronted, with double-curved pedestals and crowns. Stacked to varying heights, these assembled cases could then produce the calculated arty impression so carefully sought. In some corner of the first floor the housewife would try to cultivate an indoor window garden with the help of planters, pot stands, and trellises. These assembled effusions of greenery caught the spirit of the decade's overdone emphasis on the floral curves of nature as they crowded plants together so densely as to make them lose their individuality and produce an effect of jumbled leaves, stalks, and blossoms suffused by window light from behind.

Behind the kitchen, either up or down a few stairs, was a back yard large enough for only a small vegetable or herb garden, a child's swing, a hammock swung from a fence post to the solitary tree, and a few pieces of outdoor furniture. In some cities a block of middle-class row houses would be backed by an alley or mews, through which ash and garbage collections were made, and facing which was a solid row of stables, sometimes with servants' quarters above. Eventually these stables became automobile garages, and, because their general location had become so desirable, they were often redone as small town houses, making the alley into a narrow residential street. When there was no alleyway, the back yard ended at the fence where the rear neighbor's yard began. Horses had to be boarded, buggies kept at livery stables, and refuse barrels had to be carried out a front basement entrance onto the street.

Upstairs the most notable innovation would be the bathroom, which in those days came no more than one to a house unless the owner were wealthy. By the 1890s, an urban bathroom would be more than a zinc-lined walnut tub. On a tiled floor would be set enameled fixtures, usually white, and not greatly different from bathroom fixtures today. Owners of

Tiled walls, an indoor water closet, running water and porcelain or enameled fixtures completed a long pilgrimage toward the essentially modern bathroom. The ornamental border on the tub helps date this fixture. (Photograph by George C. Boldt, 1902)

older fixtures were urged by paint companies to cover their outdatedness with applied enamel. Early bathrooms, often converted from bedrooms, tended to be much larger than most such rooms today, but their only strange feature would be the hot-water heater suspended between the tub and basin.

Bedrooms now began to be built without fireplaces and with large clothes closets and thus came to resemble very closely the rooms most of us sleep in today. One remnant of earlier days was the washstand. With indoor plumbing it need no longer hold a chamber pot, but with only one bathroom the members of a family still counted on washing out of pitcher and bowl. The arts and crafts movement produced hexagonal dressing tables with revolving mirrors, washstands with three-sided curtain rails, beds with built-in headboards decorated with brilliant cretonne. The mood for hanging

Heavy bedroom furniture complemented by swags of fringed brocade was popular in wealthy homes of the midcentury, but began to give way to simpler furnishings by the '90s. (Photograph of Morse-Libby House, Portland, Maine, Historic American Buildings Survey)

cloth in bedrooms was powerful; a household magazine recommended twenty-one yards of dimity for draping bed, washstand, and two windows. The canopy bed returned to favor, and the space between the mattress and the floor was also draped. Bolsters—long cylindrical pillows—were widely used, and on the made-up bed could be tossed any number of occasional pillows that had not found a place in the living room. Children were encouraged to "do up" their bedrooms by hanging fashion prints from *Godey's Lady's Book,* college pennants, arts studies and autumn leaves. Centrally heated, bedrooms could be lived in as well as merely slept in; and these rooms began to show their increased use by becoming more fully furnished, more thoughtfully decorated, and more softly suggestive of leisure.

Most row houses of this era would have a fully finished third floor whose use would vary widely. In the big brownstone row houses the third floor was often a modest ballroom and the center of family entertaining. In slightly less wealthy homes, the third floor sometimes served as servants' quarters. In smaller homes, where servants in residence were not anticipated, the third floor might house a guest bedroom, a sewing room, and at least one large room, lined with cedar if possible, that took the place of the attic.

Under this attic lived a family which differed in size and nature from its counterpart in a small town thirty years earlier. The size of the average household had declined through this era, with city families showing the least inclination to reproduce themselves. A prediction of one child—or at most, two—would be likely. On the eve of the automobile age, when family feelings were still strong, there might still be an older relative living in the home. The chances of this would be less in the city of the 1890s than in the town of the 1860s, since public institutions had begun to offer alternatives to taking relatives into the home. It is impossible to imagine anyone with the status of the small-town or rural "hired girl" in a home such as this one. Although the continuing wave of immigration included large numbers of potential serving girls, the women's magazines were prone to pity the housewife for the poor quality of the help she could hire. Many of these girls were unfamiliar with the way in which an American housewife wanted her cooking done and her house run; as soon as a housewife had educated a girl to her ways, she might find that the girl had deserted her for the improved wages in factory or store. Most middle-class homes of this era had at least some domestic help, but help was becoming less regular and less dependable. Fortunately, this situation was balanced by improved household conveniences whose appearance caused husbands, unforgivably, to chide their wives on their soft life as compared with grandmother and to ask why indeed a servant was needed at all.

Day began in this home with an alarm bell instead of the crow of the back-yard rooster. On winter mornings the house would be cool, but not cold, since the furnace fire would have been glowing quietly all night and the house would have retained much of its heat. Father's first act would be the descent to the basement, where he would rattle the furnace grate to break up the banked fire and throw on new coals. Having turned up the gas flame under the water tank in the bathroom, he would return there to shave and wash as his own father had done by the kitchen stove. Meanwhile, the Irish or German maid would have arrived, changed her clothes in a basement room, entered the kitchen, lit the gas range and begun to prepare the first meal of the day.

Breakfast for a city family of the 1890s was apt to be less hearty but more varied than a rural breakfast then or earlier. Many families had begun to rely chiefly on cooked breakfast foods—oatmeal, farina—which they would vary by serving with milk and figs, strawberries, or other fruits. Those who expected meat were served chipped beef, chopped raw beef, lamb or pork chops. Eggs and codfish, creamed or in cakes, were considered adequate meat substitutes. To make breakfast more appetizing, the Boston Cooking School suggested, among other things, beef cutlets with lattice potatoes, eggs shirred in tomatoes, poached eggs with creamed celery, baked apples with gluten cereal, or a variety of breads and muffins. Sophisticated families, copying continental customs, substituted wines for coffee and made breakfast a rather formal meal. Enough businessmen had adopted the practice of inviting associates to their homes for "business breakfasts" that etiquette books had to remind their readers that only close friends could suitably appear at this intimate meal presided over by the housewife in morning dress.

From a typical row house the children could walk to grammar school, although a trolley ride might be necessary to put them at the high-school steps. Only rarely could the breadwinner walk to his place of business in the city, al-

Delmonico's, in its turn-of-the-century location, was the site not only of business lunches which shook the financial world but of gala evenings which shook the social world. (Photograph by Detroit Publishing Co., 1905)

though his trolley ride was much shorter than that of his fellow citizen who had retreated to the suburbs. The fact of commuting, coupled with the city's shorter lunch hours, meant that the family dispersed after breakfast to reconvene only in the evening. Children and their workingmen fathers carried lunch pails. Businessmen took their lunch at the saloon where a five-cent beer was the price of admission to a buffet counter of cold meats, hard-boiled eggs, sausages, and pickles. If they wished to impress a potential customer, they took him to lunch at one of the many expensive restaurants which were springing up in business districts all over urban America, all more or less modeled on Delmonico's of New York, which enjoyed the reputation of being the best and the most expensive. Between the extremes of Delmonico's and the free lunch, there also emerged the short-order houses whose noontime chaos inspired this 1896 description of "The Park Row Beanery" "Where thousands munch a hasty lunch, pay 10 cents each and go":

> With crash and smash and splash and slash the waiters
> sling the food
> And sing and yell like merry hell, so's to be understood:
> "Ham and!" "Draw one!" "Brown Wheats!" . . . "Pork 'n'
> boston!"

What happened in the home between the departure and return of the father and children depended not only on the family's solution to the servant problem but even more basically on whether the housewife were "old-fashioned" or "emancipated." Realizing that the conduct of an 1890s row house might be very similar to that of an 1860s small-town home, we might further our sense of contrast by imagining a housewife who took full advantage of what the city offered by way of freeing her from her traditional chores and routines. If she chose, she might completely disperse the old predictability of the women's world. No longer would steaming tubs signal Mondays, heated irons Tuesdays, and baking pastries Saturdays. Nor would harvesttime necessarily mean canning and spring the uprooting of rugs and furniture.

Instead, the days might seem very much like one another. The maid, having started breakfast, would disappear upstairs to close windows, make the aired beds, dust and sweep. After the family's departure she would clear the breakfast table and wash the dishes in hot water from the kitchen tank. Turning to her downstairs cleaning chores, she would find fewer crowded shelves of knickknacks to dust, furniture less pocked with lacy dirt-gathering crevices and whorls, and floor matting and linoleum which yielded up their dirt much more readily than the thick carpets and soft-grained woods of the older home. What carpets there were could be attacked with a new invention called a carpet sweeper, which was not nearly so effective as the later vacuum cleaners but which offered an improvement over the dust-scattering broom. Many homemakers were beginning to feel that, with regular attention and careful use of soaps, oils, waxes, and polishes, the house could be kept clean enough to avoid the annual purge of a thorough spring cleaning.

The greatest boon to the women's morning came with the repeal of the noonday dinner whose preparation had for-

The kitchen maid sometimes worried about watered milk, but the household began to enjoy home deliveries of almost all foodstuffs. (Engraving in *Harper's Weekly*, July 16, 1859)

merly involved both wife and help for a major part of each
day. Now only a lunch for preschool children, servants, and
the wife herself must be prepared, and this tended to be a
simple meal indeed. Food leftover from last night's dinner
might provide most of it. Cold luncheons, approved by the
housewife's guides, recommended sandwiches, cold chicken,
fruit, cottage cheese, and custard served with cold coffee or
cocoa. With only lunches such as these to think of, and with
a larger and more efficient icebox at her disposal, the housewife could easily postpone her shopping till late in the day or
could even manage for two or three days without any serious
marketing at all. Though she had no cow in the back yard,
she did have daily deliveries from the dairy farmer outside
town who ladled milk from his great cans into a jug brought
out to the curb by the maid. The baker, too, had a horse-
drawn van which called each morning, and, though many
families surrendered home-baked bread reluctantly, the
emancipated housewife called on the baker to relieve her of
part of her burdens. To the procession of milk, ice, and
bakery wagons was added in season the cart of the itinerant
greengrocer who called his wares in a melodious voice often
strongly colored with an old-world accent. A man with his
own truck garden near the city or perhaps an early visitor to
the city's great open markets, he brought corn, melons, berries, beans and peas on a fairly predictable basis. Only staples, condiments, and meats remained to be bought at the
store; and, if she cared to send a list with the maid and trust
the clerk's selection, the housewife could complete her shopping with the arrival of the delivery boy. In fact, as the use of
telephones spread, she could phone in her order and have it
"sent around right away"!

The great unsolved domestic problem was what to do with
the family wash. Mechanical washers and wringers had improved since the 1860s, but they were still arduous and un-
dependable. A stout-armed Irish maid, complained the
housewife, could break washing machines at the rate of one a

DEPOT 24 CORTLANDT ST., NEW YORK.
DEPOT, 13 BARCLAY ST., NEW YORK.

This 1869 lithograph depicted a hopeful scene of washday happiness in the home; in truth, there was considerable doubt as to the worth of home washers throughout the century.

week. Other servants, out of ignorance and fear, refused to use them at all. To this problem the progressive answer was the commercial laundry which had, by the 1890s, benefited from the development of heavy machinery and the application of steam—subsequently electric—power. Although notorious for the way they shredded fabrics and devoured buttons, commercial laundries prospered as the lesser of evils; and by the end of the century they had made Mondays bearable for many women who, if they cared to, could have their washing done while they waited.

Thus liberated from the daily tyranny of the scrub brush and market basket, and from the weekly drudgery of the laundry tub, the housewife could order her days and weeks more nearly to suit her own desires. With a smaller family and with children who spent longer days and more years in school, she could herself begin to participate in activities for which her own increased education had fitted her. Her mornings might be spent perusing one of the new variety of alert women's magazines for hints on dress and cuisine, for advice on health and behavior. She might easily find herself caught in one of the religious and sentimental novels which claimed large audiences of female readers, perhaps preparing her report for the afternoon meeting of the literary society. If her window garden did not need tending, she might turn to her needle and sewing machine, for sewing was one occupation which combined the old virtues of housewifery with the new interest in arts and crafts. Since more and more clothes were being bought from tailors and department stores, she might not be working on anything more ambitious than the inevitable darning and mending. There were, however, all those pillows to be contrived and embroidered, bright chintz to be made into furniture covers, patterned cretonne for washstand curtains, and perhaps an old muff from the third-floor

From humble beginnings (see page 124) the soda fountain became a major institution in its own right. Scores of spigots and wells made this turn-of-the-century creation a monument to variety of taste as well as marble elegance. (Photograph by Manz, 1907)

closet which, with the addition of a velvet bow, would lend a fashionably antiquarian flair to her evening costume. If she had a daughter, she might be overdoing her sewing; one lady editor complained that the modern housewife was misusing her new leisure by spending it dressing her children like French dolls.

Midday might find the mother invited to a friend's home, or attending a group luncheon at a restaurant or hotel. On those days when it was her turn to have the card club for lunch, she would spend the morning supervising the table setting and coaching the forgetful maid on the niceties of service. The meal would be light; but it would have several courses, each prepared with great care. For, along with decorative sewing, imaginative cooking had been elevated to a high and decorative art, often revealing the same breadth of foreign influence observable in the living-room furnishings. A clear soup would be followed by a fish course—stuffed haddock, chartreuse of salmon—served in dainty portions. Broiled chops with fresh peas, followed by a lettuce salad dressed at the table and eaten with cream cheese and wafers, then ladyfingers and whipped cream preceded the coffee at one representative luncheon. Some of the central dishes were elaborate both visually and culinarily. A scallop salad, for example, called for boiled and marinated scallops being mixed with celery and mayonnaise, and formed into a mound. Capers were used to outline designs on the sides of the mound, and the designs were filled with red and white garnishing made from chopped beets and egg whites. Before this monument was placed on the table, it was to be crowned with bright spinach leaves and surrounded with radishes rosetted and flower-shaped cuts of celery.

Afternoons might be spent with groups of ladies gathered for serious or recreational purposes, listening to a lecture, attending a matinee, visiting a gallery or an antique shop. The arrival of the children from school would begin to turn the day back toward more domestic patterns, as supervised homework was begun. Usually there was some grocery shopping to be done and the preparations for the evening meal to be overseen; but, with the length of the trolley trip extending the husband's working day, the housewife had more time to prepare for the assembling of the family around the evening dinner table.

It was this occasion that came closest to resembling the rather formal noontime ritual of earlier days. Less eager to impress her family than her female friends, the housewife served them less ornate food in greater quantities. In spite of the fact that nutrition was becoming a profession and diet a preoccupation, these meals would have seemed hearty and uninhibited in their generous quantities of fish, roast meats, potatoes and breads. With the rise of commercial refrigeration and the canned-goods revolution, the city cook of the 1890s could spread her table with a greater variety of fruits and vegetables, fresh and cooked. The accepted convenience of the icebox, sometimes set on casters to be rolled into the dining room, made a new fad of cold desserts, including ice cream. At the head of this bountiful table sat the father; and, if he were not quite the symbol of authority his father had been, neither were the children so liberated as theirs were to become. Mother, better educated and more conscious of her position as a family leader, shared the conversation, the decision-making, and the establishment of family rules of behavior. Children were still expected to know their place and to speak when spoken to.

At the end of the meal, however, the family group no longer adjourned en masse to surround the living-room table. Young girls sat on the front steps with their nearby friends; boys leap-frogged over ash cans or looked for enough others to pick up a game of baseball in the street or in a nearby park or vacant lot. If father were not off to a lodge meeting, he would take his cigar and the evening paper into the living room or den, either of which he might have completely to himself. There were still evenings around the piano, stereopticons, games of Authors and checkers. A new "Coxey's Army Puzzle" revealed a reflection in parlor games of current events, this one a march of the unemployed on Washington in 1894. The lure of urban diversions, however, made quiet evenings at home less frequent. City couples spent more time in strictly adult company, entertaining and being entertained in each other's homes, or attending music halls, dances, and stage events.

Days ended with a gradual dispersal of the characters. Having finished the dinner dishes, the maid would be off for her own home at the other end of the trolley line. Children, their lessons and play exhausted, made their way independently to bed. For mother and daughter, however, the routine of retiring might consume considerable time and energy; for this was an era not only of endlessly brushed tresses but also of beauty and health regimens. Mild exercises were recommended for women whose leisure might adversely affect their health; various soaps and cosmetics competed in the pages of women's magazines for the essential place in madame's beauty routines; pundits with letters after their names wrote columns urging deep breathing, daily bathing in cold water, and beauty sleep before midnight. While his wife was compulsively opening the bedroom windows from both top and bottom, the husband would perform the final chores: locking the doors, putting out the cat, checking to see that all the gas jets were off, and lastly, in winter, banking the furnace fire to last the night.

Weekdays the whole family might assemble only at breakfast and dinner; but the opportunities for working, playing, and praying together were augmented by new weekend routines. Saturday was considered very much a family day, with children home from school and with more and more business concerns closing at noon. During the morning, mother would supervise the children's chores. A daughter might be put to washing gaslight mantles, polishing silver, or giving her closet a special cleaning. For a boy there would be ashes to haul up from the furnace, a yard to be picked up, a garden to be weeded or snow to be swept. If his mother had only part-time servants he might even—shame to say it—help with the heavier cleaning. In the afternoon there would be time for skating, sledding, baseball, swimming, or playing with marbles or dolls, depending on age, sex, and season.

Sundays would center on church just as surely if not so extensively in city as in town. Services began later and were attended by packed congregations of very carefully turned-out families who often found the intellectual climax of their week in what was said from the pulpit of the socially conscious urban minister. The morning service would have been lengthy and might have been further attenuated by Sunday School or Bible Class before or after; but evening services, although they were still customarily offered, were not attended so compulsively as they were in smaller communities. The greatest contrast, however, was between the arrested motion of the strict small-town Sabbath and the bustle of the city corrupted by the "continental Sabbath" of exuberant recreation. This was the day the German immigrants flocked to their beer gardens for music and dancing, setting what many considered a sacrilegious precedent. In the city, however, the prospect of so many people enjoying themselves so thoroughly was too much for even Victorian Puritanism to resist. Soon stores and places of amusement were staying open Sundays, and, except in areas where fundamentalist religious views predominated, the day became one of care-free entertainment, outdoors if possible. There were zoos and amusement parks to be visited; lakes for skating in winter and boating in summer; tennis, baseball, and golf to be played or watched; and fine places to dine.

Furthermore, as Saturday became decreasingly a full day of work, the concept of the recreational weekend began to emerge. The train, the excursion boat, the bicycle, and even the interurban trolley had given families the mobility for two-day trips that would have been difficult with horse-drawn transportation. Resorts began to flourish within easy reach of the cities, often at the end of specially built rail lines. Beaches, mineral springs, golf courses, and mountain scenery provided the principal drawing cards for these weekend hotels which have now been swallowed up by the cities they used to serve at a formidable distance. With the coming of the private motor car, the idea of the weekend excursion became so irresistible as to threaten even the habit of church attendance; but the pattern for this new departure was formed while automobiles were still a rarity.

As the weekend provided a predictable break in daily routines, so the summer season came to vary the patterns of other seasons, and in much the same way. The newly urbanized American, uncomfortable among the cast iron and asphalt, exhibited an unmistakable nostalgia for the openness of the natural environment whence he probably came; and, as weekends sent him to the nearby resorts, so summers propelled him to a primitive retreat beside some cooling stream or bay. Middle-class city dwellers, including many who could not afford it, owned summer homes within a half-day's trip from the city; and vacation centers on Cape Cod, the Jersey shore, Long Island, and the southern lakes of Wisconsin grew up to serve Boston, Philadelphia, New York, and Chicago respectively. Builders sold portable cottages, and magazines featured model plans for summer retreats. Even fathers whose business kept them in the city all summer would insist on the healthful benefits of rusticating the wife and children. The mother, unless she had been lucky enough to persuade the maid to come along, would then have the opportunity of coping with the daily problems of housekeeping under conditions more reminiscent of her grandmother's farm than of her own home in the city. For some reason—perhaps for the joy of watching the children grow tan and learn to swim— the wife accepted this opportunity to keep house with full handicap. At least she could tell her troubles to her husband during his weekend visits.

Besides refreshing themselves with regular returns to nature, the city family broke the monotony of daily routines by enthusiastically celebrating a number of holidays. None revealed the sentimental side of this era better than St. Valentine's Day, which in some communities was rivaled only by Christmas in importance. Then, as now, the central ritual was the tendering of cards and gifts to loved ones. Commercial valentines had been introduced early in the nineteenth century, but they reached a height of elaborate elegance during the Age of Enterprise. Many a lover hand-made his token of affection and copied painstakingly, in the flowing script of the day, an original ode to his beloved. The lithographer Prang, with the shrewdness that characterized his reading of public taste throughout these years, brought out a gaudy line of cards priced from 5 cents to $3, which shopkeepers displayed in their windows as early as January. Lavishly ornate, the most prized of these cards were trimmed with silk or lace

On Christmas Eve in 1898 children were dreaming of horse-drawn steam fire engines, destroyers modeled on the "Great White Fleet" of the U. S. Navy, "safety" bikes with racing handlebars, and the inevitable dolls, drums, and stuffed animals. (Lithograph by Strobridge)

and included ornaments of spun glass, mother-of-pearl, and imitation jewels. One enterprising merchant offered to deliver cards and gifts purchased at his store in a Valentine Express, drawn by eight horses, which raced from house to house all day long. A minority reaction to all this sweetness took the form of "vinegar valentines," crude anonymous messages sent on cheap paper; but popular opinion decried the bad taste of these satires.

Valentine parties were very much in vogue in smart urban circles, making this one of the few holidays which brought guests from outside the family into the home. Hostesses were urged to spare no effort in making these parties as memorably original as possible. Endless variations of designs based on Cupids, hearts, and bows graced the living rooms. Another theme for such entertainments was based on the legend that February 14 was the day on which birds chose their mates. Thus a hostess might invite each couple to come dressed as a specific variety of bird; the assembled guests rivaled Noah in the panorama of paired species. At such an affair the refreshment table would be trimmed with sticks

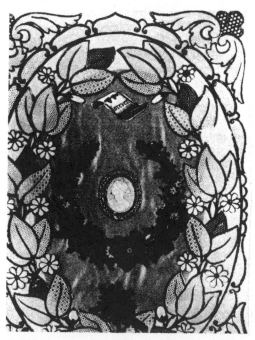

Probably made in about 1890 with obvious loving care, this valentine featured real lace insets and a genuine cameo in its center.

and straw to resemble a nest, and the food itself would be served in paper eggs. In such observances might lie a clue as to why St. Valentine's Day has not maintained its full glory in the present century.

The celebration of New Year's Day showed a transition from old to new ways. The midcentury custom required that a family state hours during which they would be at home on January 1. A table was laid with cold meats, pastries, the traditional eggnog, and a bowl of the host's favorite punch. During the announced interval the family would expect all their friends to call, partake of food and drink, and exchange New Year felicitations. The family must, in its turn, pay calls during their friends' announced hours. So the day became crowded with carriages vying for space in the streets, rushing frantically lest a neglected visit result in an offended friend. Less conscientious strollers sampled any handy bowl, invited or not, and long before evening the urban streets would echo wavering song and unsteady footsteps.

As cities grew and friends lived farther and farther apart, the day became an increasingly hectic and decreasingly enjoyable series of hurried calls. The first retreat from custom came when callers began only to leave cards, knowing that the host would himself be away depositing his own calling cards. The second step came when families hired someone to deliver their cards, or mailed them; finally, by the turn of the century, these frantic visits had been generally abandoned. In their place came the parade. In 1876, Philadelphia's Silver Crown New Year's Association marched from the Centennial Grounds to Independence Hall where they were joined by other bands dressed as harlequins, princes, squaws, and animals. This annual procession grew until it was made an official city function at the turn of the century, by which time the "Mummer's Parade," as it was called, had become widely known and imitated. Pasadena, in 1886, for the first time saw a procession of flower-bedecked carriages following a

Of the many great holiday parades, none was more consistently imposing than St. Patrick's Day in New York. (Lithograph by Thomas Kelly after a drawing by Lucian Gray, 1874)

prearranged route to the site of an athletic contest, a precedent which developed into the Tournament of Roses.

The parade was becoming for the city dweller the holiday equivalent of the picnic for the small-town resident. In 1870 Irish immigrants in Los Angeles organized the first of many St. Patrick's Day parades. Peter J. McGuire, president of the United Brotherhood of Carpenters and Joiners and a man who had doubtless marched on many St. Patrick's Days, proposed in 1882 that Labor Day in New York City be commemorated with a grand march; and thus began another precedent for floats and drums. Americans had been marching on the Fourth of July since they won the right to celebrate that day, and these pageants grew suitably elaborate, especially in New England, as the century grew older.

At one end of the parade route stood a battery of orators. Holiday celebrants in city and town counted on them for a display of rhetoric sufficiently florid to distract from sore feet and thirsty throats and to fill all hearts with the glory of the occasion. Today, when oratory has become one of the lost arts, it is hard to appreciate how often these famous speakers —none greater than William Jennings Bryan—succeeded in exhilarating audiences who already knew what they were going to hear and who stood crowded together, heavily dressed beneath a burning sun, with children tugging insistently at their waists or crying impatiently in their arms, removed by fifty yards from a voice which used only its natural powers of amplification. When the last metaphorical eagle had soared from the last speaker's lips, all were rewarded with cold lemonade or beer; but, rewards aside, these marathon memorializers of Independence and the Laboring Man must be considered—along with their listeners—as heroes of a departed day.

The inevitable life processes which colored home life in the midcentury rural home affected the city family just as inexorably but had to a great extent moved outside the home. Courtship, for example, had moved from the front-parlor sofa to a wrought-iron chair in the corner ice-cream parlor. Here the young couple hesitated longingly before making their choice from a bewildering variety of ices and syrups dispensed from shining marble soda fountains made to delight the eye as well as the palate. Many outdoor sports— archery, tennis, golf—permitted mingling of the sexes, as did the theaters and restaurants of the city. Conventions of courtship were still sedate. A young couple could walk together unchaperoned, but when riding they needed at least the company of a coachman to be proper. Visits to homes were still important, but they had lost their central position in the courtship process.

Engagements and weddings were much more elaborate in

city than in town and fraught with pitfalls of impropriety which etiquette manuals and women's magazines labored to avoid. A formal engagement announcement and party was expected; but, unless the bride's parents owned a large home, they would use the facilities of the country club or the hotel ballroom, as they would for the wedding reception as well. Wedding banquets and bridal trousseaus were no less pretentious; but, instead of involving the women in weeks of labor, they might be solved with a call to the hotel caterer and a series of visits to the bridal department of the clothing store. The bride had to be very careful about wording invitations precisely and mailing them exactly two weeks prior to the event; nor dared she fail to acknowledge even the slightest wedding gift with a note and a small bouquet.

When the couple returned from the honeymoon and settled down, they would be favored with a number of polite dinner invitations which they would not be expected to return immediately, especially if they were among the many who started married life in boarding houses. With the appearance of the first child, the couple would begin searching for an apartment or house of their own, and soon they would begin to even the social score. The birth of a child, especially the first, was anticipated still by the accumulation of a fancy layette; but if the items were not family heirlooms, they would more likely have come from a department store than from the expectant mother's knitting needles. As the confinement time drew near, the doctor would prepare his patient for delivery and recuperation in a hospital rather than in the home.

The treatment of sickness and death was also becoming more modern; that is, more dependent on doctors, nurses, hospitals, and funeral parlors than on the family and the neighbors. The solicitous practices of the 1860s had by no means disappeared, but the city habits of the 1890s were much closer to what we would find natural today. Funerals were still more ceremonially ornate, with the resplendant

black-plumed hearse symbolizing the attenuated lugubrious-
ness of the services. Mourning dress and armbands were
faithfully worn for prescribed periods: for wives or husbands,
two years; for parents, brothers and sisters, one; and so on
down the line to first cousins, who were mourned for one
month. Arguments against the heavy crepe veil and ruffles
were heard on grounds of health and practicality, but the
punctilious observance of form was expected here as in other
matters.

The source of this rigorous training in decorum was the
home. Compared with the home of the 1860s, that of the
'90s may have been much less of a schoolhouse of practical
behavior, but it was more rather than less a school of etiquette. In polite urban homes of the '90s etiquette was no
simple matter, as suggested by the customs surrounding holidays, weddings, and funerals. Just how extensively rigid rules
of conduct reached into situations where ritual hardly exists
today may be gathered from the following extract, published
in a popular middle-class magazine of the day:

Society asks little of a young man except to behave well.
If he be manly in looks, if he has a good manner, is civil to
his elders, if he has any little gift of entertaining—any
"parlor tricks"—if he sends a few flowers occasionally,
looks pleasant and is polite, his way will be smooth to
success—always providing that he is really a gentleman.

When a son has lately entered society his mother leaves
his card with her husband's upon her acquaintances. He
will then be included in the season's general invitations.

He pays his first calls preferably upon formal receiving
days until he has won his way to a more cordial reception
and is invited for dinner, theatre or other limited hos-
pitality. He is then upon friendly footing and may show
some reciprocal attention if he please. A man is never
invited to dine where he has not previously called.

Men leave their cards early in the season if they wish to

be included in the round of its festivities. A call after any civility received is the proper courtesy.

The lady always gives the invitation to call. A man must not go beyond an evident pleasure in her society by way of suggestion. Sometimes a woman friend will exert herself for him. The sooner the call follows the invitation the greater the compliment. A fortnight is the usual interval.

A "roof introduction" establishes no claim to future recognition unless the lady acknowledge the acquaintance by bow or smile when they next meet. If at a ball he may then approach and ask her to dance.

Although the family was still unquestionably the important social unit, it was beginning to lose the dominance it had enjoyed at midcentury. Girls were no longer spending their afternoons at their mothers' sides during school years, then helping patiently at home until marriage made them housewives themselves. Instead they were finishing high school, even going to college and professional schools, and diluting home ties with aims and desires formed and kindled outside. If marriage did not overtake them early, they would leave home anyway to live in boarding houses or small apartments and begin their own careers. Boys exhibited even more independence. A small-town father in the 1860s was doubtless pleased when a well-behaved son came down to the store to learn the trade and follow in his father's footsteps. The urban father of the '90s hoped that his son would go on to college, enjoy the advantages of an education he himself had probably never known, and display these advantages by surpassing his father in every way. If it is, as some have observed, a trait of American fathers to want their sons to outdo them—grow taller, get better grades in school, attend better colleges, make more money and move in better circles—then the fathers of the 1890s exhibited this trait most emphatically.

Suggestions for Further Reading

These books were selected with several criteria in mind: that they be readable, available and, if possible, meaningfully illustrated; that they reflect contemporary attitudes of the Age of Enterprise; and that they include the works on which this one relied most heavily.

GENERAL

Adams, Henry, *Education of Henry Adams*. Boston: Houghton Mifflin Co., 1918.

Adams, James T., *et al., Album of American History* (especially volumes III and IV). New York: Charles Scribner's Sons, 1944–60.

Botkin, Benjamin A., ed., *Treasury of American Folklore*. New York: Crown Publisher, Inc., 1944.

Brown, Richard C., *Human Side of American History*. Boston: Ginn and Co., 1962.

Diamond, Sigmund, ed., *Nation Transformed* (document collection). New York: George Braziller, Inc., 1963.

Gabriel, Ralph H., ed., *Pageant of America, a Pictorial History of the United States*, 15 vols. New Haven: Yale University Press, 1925–29.

Nevins, Allan, *Emergence of Modern America, 1865–1878.* New York: The Macmillan Company, 1928.

Schlesinger, Arthur M., *Rise of the City, 1878–1898*. New York: The Macmillan Company, 1933.

Walker, Robert H., *Poet and the Gilded Age*. Philadelphia: University of Pennsylvania Press, 1963.

Wish, Harvey, *Society and Thought in Modern America*, Vol. II, *Society and Thought in America,* 2nd ed. New York: David McKay Co., Inc., 1962.

CHAPTER ONE: VILLAGE HOME AND FAMILY: 1860s

Anon., *Art of Good Behavior: Being a Complete Guide to the Usages of Polite Society*. New York: Fisher, 1879.

Atherton, Lewis E., *Main Street on the Middle Border*. Bloomington: Indiana University Press, 1954.

Deming, Maria R. [Mrs. Oakey], *From Attic to Cellar, a Book for Young Housekeepers*. New York: G. P. Putnam's Sons, 1879.

George, William D., *American Book of Days*. New York: H. W. Wilson Co., 1937.

Howe, Edgar W., *Story of a Country Town*. Boston: Houghton Mifflin Co., 1884.

Langdon, William C., *Everyday Things in American Life, 1607–1876*, 2 vols. New York: Charles Scribner's Sons, 1941.

Lavin, Elizabeth M., *Homemaking and Housekeeping*. New York: Butterick, 1889.

Richards, Caroline C., *Village Life in America, 1852–1872*. New York: Holt, Rinehart, and Winston, 1913.

Stowe, Harriet B. and Catherine E. Beecher, *American Woman's Home*. New York: Ford, 1869.

Thompson, Slason. *Way Back When: Recollection of an Octogenarian, 1849–1929*. Chicago: Kroch, 1931.

CHAPTER TWO: THE IMPACT OF TECHNOLOGY

Adams, Charles F. and Henry, *Chapters of the Erie*. Boston: Osgood, 1871.

Beebe, Lucius M. and Charles Clegg. *When Beauty Rode the Rails*. New York: Doubleday & Co., Inc., 1962.

Bryan, George S., *Edison, the Man and his Works*. New York: Alfred A. Knopf, 1926.

Burlingame, Roger, *Engines of Democracy, Inventions and Society in Mature America*. New York: Charles Scribner's Sons, 1940.

Carnegie, Andrew, *Autobiography of Andrew Carnegie*. Boston: Houghton Mifflin Co., 1920.

Kaempffert, Waldemar B., ed., *Popular History of American Invention*. New York: Charles Scribner's Sons, 1924.

Lauer, Conrad N., *Engineering in American Industry*. New York: McGraw-Hill Book Co., 1924.

Moody, John, *Railroad Builders*. New Haven: Yale University Press, 1919.

Oliver, John W., *History of American Technology*. New York: Ronald Press Co., 1956.

Thompson, Slason, *Short History of American Railways*. Chicago: Bureau of Railway News and Statistics, 1925.

CHAPTER THREE: LIFE ON FARM AND FRONTIER

Adams, Andy, *Log of a Cowboy*. Boston: Houghton Mifflin Co., 1927.

Betzinez, Jason, with Wilbur S. Nye, *I Fought with Geronimo*. Harrisburg, Pa.: Stackpole Co., 1959.

Carson, Gerald, *Old Country Store*. New York: Oxford University Press, 1954.

Dick, Everett N., *Sodhouse Frontier, 1854–1890*. New York: Appleton-Century, 1937.

Dodd, Helen, *Healthful Farmhouse*. Boston: Whitcomb and Barrows, 1906.

Garland, Hamlin, *Son of the Middle Border*. New York: The Macmillan Company, 1917.

Macrae, David, *Americans at Home*. Edinburgh: Edmonston and Douglas, 1870.

Nordhoff, Charles, *Cotton States in the Spring and Summer of 1875*. New York: Appleton, 1876.

Shinn, Charles H., *Mining Camps, A Study in American Frontier*

Government. Baltimore: Johns Hopkins University Press, 1884.

Washington, Booker T., *Up from Slavery*. New York: Burt, 1901.

CHAPTER FOUR: THE CHANGING COMMUNITY

Addams, Jane, *Twenty Years at Hull House*. New York: The Macmillan Company, 1910.

Andrews, Wayne, *Architecture, Ambition and Americans*. New York: Harper & Row, 1955.

Butler, Nicholas M., ed., *Education in the United States*, 2 vols. Albany: Lyon, 1900.

Byrn, Edward W., *Progress of Invention in the Nineteenth Century*. New York: Munn, 1900.

Green, Samuel S., *Public Library Movement in the United States, 1853–1893*. Boston: Boston Book, 1913.

Masters, Edgar L., *Spoon River Anthology*. New York: The Macmillan Company, 1915.

Parkhurst, Charles H., *Our Fight with Tammany*. New York: Charles Scribner's Sons, 1895.

Riis, Jacob A., *How the Other Half Lives*. New York: Charles Scribner's Sons, 1890.

Sheldon, Henry D., *Student Life and Customs*. New York: Appleton, 1901.

Walling, George W., *Recollections of a New York Chief of Police*. New York: Caxton, 1887.

Wecter, Dixon, *Saga of American Society*. New York: Charles Scribner's Sons, 1937.

White, William A., *Autobiography*. New York: The Macmillan Company, 1946.

CHAPTER FIVE: LEISURE AND POPULAR TASTE

Blair, Walter, ed., *Native American Humor (1800–1900)*. New York: American Book Publishing Co., 1931.

Crawford, Mary C., *Romance of the American Theatre*. Boston: Little, Brown, and Co., 1925.

Davidson, Marshall B., *Life in America*, 2 vols. Boston: Houghton Mifflin Co., 1951.

Davies, Wallace E., *Patriotism on Parade: the Story of Veterans' and Hereditary Organizations in America, 1783–1900.* Cambridge: Harvard University Press, 1955.

Dulles, Foster R., *America Learns to Play: A History of Popular Recreation, 1607–1940.* New York: Peter Smith Publisher, 1952.

Fehlandt, August F., *Century of Drink Reform in the United States.* Cincinnati: Jennings and Graham, 1904.

Irwin, Inez, *Angels and Amazons: a Hundred Years of American Women.* New York: Doubleday, Doran, 1933.

Lynes, Russell, *Tastemakers.* New York: Harper & Row, 1954.

Mott, Frank L., *Golden Multitudes: the Story of Best Sellers in the United States.* New York: R. R. Bowker Co., 1947.

Mumford, Lewis, *Brown Decades: a Study of the Arts in America, 1865–1895.* New York: Harcourt, Brace, 1931.

Spaeth, Sigmund, *History of Popular Music in America.* New York: Random House, 1948.

CHAPTER SIX: THE AGE OF THE PERIODICAL

Hower, Ralph M., *History of an Advertising Agency.* Cambridge: Harvard University Press, 1939.

Jones, Edgar R., *Those Were the Good Old Days: A Happy Look at American Advertising, 1880–1930,* New York: Simon and Schuster, 1959.

Mott, Frank L., *American Journalism.* New York: The Macmillan Company, 1940.

———. *History of American Magazines.* Vol. III (1865–85) and Vol. IV (1885–1905). Cambridge: Harvard University Press, 1938, 1957.

Nevins, Allan, *American Press Opinion.* Boston: D. C. Heath and Co., 1928.

Paine, Albert B., *Th. Nast: His Period and His Pictures.* New York: Harper & Row, 1904.

Park, Robert E., *Immigrant Press and Its Control.* New York: Harper & Row, 1922.

Steffens, J. Lincoln, *Autobiography.* New York: Harcourt, Brace, 1931.

Wood, James P., *Magazines in the United States: Their Social and Economic Influence.* New York: Ronald Press Co., 1949.

CHAPTER SEVEN: URBAN HOME AND FAMILY: 1890s

Allen, Edith, *Mechanical Devices in the Home*. Peoria: Manual Arts, 1922.

Armstrong, Hamilton F., *Those Days*. New York: Harper & Row, 1963.

Bouton, Emily S., *Social Etiquette,* 7th ed. Chicago: Neely, 1894.

Faulkner, Harold U., *Politics, Reform and Expansion, 1890–1900*. New York: Harper & Row, 1959.

Ormsbee, Thomas H., *Field Guide to American Victorian Furniture*. Boston: Little, Brown and Co., 1951.

Putnam, George H., *Memories of a Publisher, 1865–1915*. New York: G. P. Putnam's Sons, 1915.

Stewart, George R., *American Ways of Life*. New York: Doubleday & Co., Inc., 1954.

Sullivan, Mark, *Our Times,* Vol. I, *Turn of the Century, 1900–1904*. New York: Charles Scribner's Sons, 1926.

Index

The Author

Born in Cincinnati, Robert H. Walker attended North-western (B.A.), Columbia (M.A.), and Pennsylvania (Ph.D.). His research and writing, including *The Poet and the Gilded Age*, has centered on the history and literature of late-19th-century America. Having taught at Carnegie Tech, Haverford, Pennsylvania, and Wyoming, Mr. Walker is now on leave from George Washington University, serving as the first director of Educational and Special Projects for the National Endowment for the Humanities.

The author lives in Washington, D.C., with his wife and their children, Amy, Rachel, and Matthew.